Testing English as a Second Language

David P. Harris

Georgetown University

McGraw-Hill Book Company

New York • St. Louis • San Francisco
London • Toronto • Sydney • Mexico • Panama

About the Author

David P. Harris is an outstanding expert in the testing of English as a second language. Since 1961 he has been Professor of Linguistics and Director of the American Language Institute of Georgetown University. He received his Ph.D. in linguistics from the University of Michigan in 1954 and has done graduate work at Stanford University and the State University of Iowa. He was a Fulbright Lecturer at the University of Athens (1957-1958) and later Coordinator of the Fulbright English Language Program in Greece and Visiting Professor of Linguistics at the Universities of Athens and Thessaloniki, Greece (1967-1968). He was a test writer with Educational Testing Service, Princeton, New Jersey (1952-1953), and the English Language Institute, University of Michigan (1954). From 1963 to 1965 he was Project Director for Testing of English as a Foreign Language (TOEFL), a program cosponsored by Educational Testing Service and the College Entrance Examination Board.

21222324252627282930   MMN MMN   9087654321

Contents

96681

Preface

Although there are now a number of very excellent textbooks on the methods of teaching English as a second language, we have lacked a short, concise text on the testing of ESL, a subject about which both classroom teachers and trainers of teachers have shown an increasing concern. It is hoped that this little book will help to meet the need by providing just about the right amount of material for the testing component of teacher-training courses and that at the same time it will prove useful for home study by teachers whose formal training slighted this important subject.

The twofold objective of the book is to enable the ESL teacher both to improve his own classroom measures and to make sound assessments of standardized tests which he may from time to time be asked to select, administer, and interpret. In the opening chapters he is introduced to the general purposes and methods of language testing and is asked to consider the chief characteristics of good educational measures. A series of six chapters then describes specific techniques for testing each of the major components of English as taught to speakers of other languages, after which attention is directed to the step-by-step process whereby the ESL test is constructed and administered, and the results interpreted. The final chapter offers procedures for calculating a few basic test statistics which will aid the teacher–test writer in evaluating the soundness of his tests and the performance of his students. As with the rest of the book, the final chapter assumes no previous training in tests and measurement and no knowledge of advanced mathematics.

In the preparation of this book, the writer drew from "sources too numerous to mention," though a small number are identified in the footnotes and in the list of selected references which appears in the back. In addition, he included material from two of his own earlier writings: the *English Testing Guidebook*, Parts I-II, prepared for the International Cooperation Administration in 1961; and the article "The Testing of Student Writing Ability," which appeared in *Reflections on High School English*, edited by Gary Tate and published by the University of Tulsa in 1966. The writer wishes to express his appreciation to Professor Tate and the University of Tulsa for permission to incorporate portions of this article in the present work.

The writer is deeply indebted to Dr. Edith Huddleston of the National Institute of Mental Health, Professor Betty W. Robinett of Ball State University, Professor Leslie A. Palmer of Georgetown University, and Mr. John Upshur of the English Language Institute, University of Michigan, for their careful reading of parts or all of the manuscript and for their extremely valuable comments and suggestions. For the material added during revision, the writer is, of course, entirely responsible.

David P. Harris

1 Purposes and Methods of Language Testing

TEACHER-MADE VERSUS STANDARDIZED TESTS

In any consideration of educational testing, a distinction must be drawn between the rather informal, teacher-made tests of the classroom and those formal, large-scale, "standardized" instruments which are prepared by professional testing services to assist institutions in the selection, placement, and evaluation of students.

Classroom tests are generally prepared, administered, and scored by one teacher. In this situation, test objectives can be based directly on course objectives, and test content derived from specific course content. Inasmuch as instructor, test writer, and evaluator are all the same individual, the students know pretty much what is expected of them—what is likely to be covered by the test questions and what kind of standards are likely to be applied in the scoring and the interpretation of results. And since the scoring will be done by only one person, the standards should remain *reasonably* consistent from paper to paper and test to test. Moreover, it is very likely that the teacher's ultimate evaluation of his students will be based on a number of tests and other measures, not just one. Therefore a single bad test performance by a student need not do irreparable damage to his final standing, nor, probably, will one inadequate or ineptly constructed test prevent the teacher from making a reasonably sound final judgment. Finally, since the number of students to be tested is relatively small, the teacher is not limited to quickly scorable item types but may, if he wishes, make full use of compositions and short-answer techniques (see below).

Obviously, few if any of the above conditions apply to the standardized test, designed to be used with thousands and sometimes hundreds of thousands of subjects throughout the nation or the world, and prepared (and perhaps administered, scored, and interpreted) by a team of testing specialists with no personal knowledge of the examinees and no opportunity to check on the consistency of individual performances.

Even though this book has been designed primarily for the classroom teacher, we shall deal throughout with both types of testing. For although the teacher's primary testing concern will be in improving his own classroom measures, he will quite probably need at some time or other to make use of standardized tests, and it is therefore important that he know how to select and evaluate such instruments as well. And, in turn, learning more about the techniques and research findings of the professional testers will help the classroom teacher to write better tests himself.

THE PRINCIPAL EDUCATIONAL USES OF LANGUAGE TESTS

Before we can even begin to plan a language test, we must establish its *purpose* or *function*. Language tests have many uses in educational programs, and quite often the same test will be used for two or more related purposes. The following list summarizes the chief objectives of language testing; the categories are not by any means mutually exclusive, but they do indicate six different *emphases* in measuring student ability or potential.

1. **To determine readiness for instructional programs**. Some screening tests are used to separate those who are prepared for an academic or training program from those who are not. Such selection tests have a single cutoff point: examinees either "pass" or "fail" the test, and the degree of success or failure may not be deemed important.

2. To classify or place individuals in appropriate language classes. Other screening tests try to distinguish *degrees of proficiency* so that examinees may be assigned to specific sections or activities on the basis of their current level of competence. Such tests may make no pass-fail distinctions, since some kind of training is offered to everyone.

3. To diagnose the individual's specific strengths and weaknesses. Diagnostic screening tests generally consist of several short but reliable subtests measuring different language skills or components of a single broad skill. On the basis of the individual's performance on each subtest, we can plot a *performance profile* which will show his relative strength in the various areas tested.

4. To measure aptitude for learning. Still another kind of screening test is used to predict future performance. At the time of testing, the examinees may have little or no knowledge of the language to be studied, and the test is employed to assess their potential.

5. To measure the extent of student achievement of the instructional goals. Achievement tests are used to indicate group or individual progress toward the instructional objectives of a specific study or training program. Examples are progress tests and final examinations in a course of study.

6. To evaluate the effectiveness of instruction. Other achievement tests are used exclusively to assess the degree of success not of individuals but of the instructional program itself. Such tests are often used in research, when experimental and "control" classes are given the same educational goals but use different materials and techniques to achieve them.

For simplicity, the foregoing six categories can be grouped under three headings: *aptitude* (category 4 above), *general proficiency* (categories 1 to 3), and *achievement* (categories 5 and 6). These three general types of language tests may be defined in the following manner:

An aptitude test serves to indicate an individual's facility for acquiring specific skills and learnings.

A general proficiency test indicates what an individual is capable of doing now (as the result of his cumulative learning experiences), though it may also serve as a basis for predicting future attainment.

An achievement test indicates the extent to which an individual has mastered the specific skills or body of information acquired in a formal learning situation.

Not all measurement specialists use this three-way division of tests or interpret the terms aptitude, proficiency, and achievement precisely as we have done above. Our three categories do, however, seem to lend themselves well to the classification of language tests and will be of value in helping us in succeeding chapters to differentiate among the principal testing objectives.

Actually, our concern in this book will be almost entirely with measures of proficiency and achievement. For although some successful attempts at developing general language aptitude tests have been made,[1] this area of testing is still relatively new, and no aptitude measures specifically for learners of English as a second language could be said to have passed the experimental stage. Valid English aptitude measures would be of inestimable value to both educational institutions and international-exchange agencies in this country, for if English-learning potential could be accepted as a substitute for current proficiency and achievement, it would then become economically feasible to admit non-English-speaking students to academic or technical-training programs that would include short-term, intensive English language components. Let it be hoped, therefore, that some of the current experimentation will soon bear fruit.

THE PRINCIPAL LANGUAGE-TESTING TECHNIQUES

Translation

Translation was formerly one of the most common teaching and testing devices, and it remains quite popular today in many parts of the world. However, with the spread of the new "linguistically oriented" methods of instruction and measurement, translation has lost much of its appeal in this country. In the first place, translation is in reality a very specialized and highly sophisticated activity, and one which neither develops nor demonstrates the basic skills of listening, speaking, reading, and writing. Indeed, the habit of

---

[1]Especially significant is John B. Carroll and Stanley M. Sapon's *Modern Language Aptitude Test,* Form A (New York: The Psychological Corporation, 1955-1958), a test designed for native speakers of English learning modern foreign languages. Adaptations in other languages are now in experimental use.

translating is now felt to *impede* the proper learning of a foreign language, for one of the first objectives in modern foreign-language instruction is to free the learner from native-language interference—to teach him to react in the target language without recourse to his mother tongue. To be sure, modern language departments often include advanced-level courses in translation, but here translation is treated as a creative activity which follows, and depends upon, fairly complete mastery of the target language. In an achievement test for translation courses, there of course would be very good reasons for having the examinees translate.

Secondly, translation is extremely difficult to evaluate. Is a "good" translation one that captures the tone and mood of the original by substituting the idiom of the second language, or is translation only "good" when it approaches a literal, word-for-word rendering of the original? The criteria and standards for judging translations depend so much on individual taste that the translation test tends to be a highly unreliable kind of measure, and particularly when large numbers of examinees require several scorers.

Dictation

Dictation is another testing device that retains some of its former popularity in certain areas. Dictation is undoubtedly a useful pedagogical device (if used in moderation) with beginning and low-intermediate-level learners of a foreign language, and the responses that such students make to dictations will certainly tell the teacher something about their phonological, grammatical, and lexical weaknesses. Other types of tests, however, provide much more complete and systematic diagnosis, and in far less time. As a testing device, then, dictation must be regarded as generally both uneconomical and imprecise.

Composition

A composition test allows the examinee to compose his own relatively free and extended written responses to problems set by the examiner. In foreign-language testing these responses may consist of single paragraphs or may be full essays in which the student is rated not only on his use of the grammatical structures and lexicon of the target language but also on his ideas and their organization. Grades for such "free-response" tests may also take into account the examinee's employment of the graphic conventions—spelling, punctuation, capitalization, paragraphing, and even handwriting.

If composition tests are somewhat less frequently employed in foreign-language courses now than formerly—at least in this country —the principal reason is probably the growing popularity of the audio-lingual method of teaching, not the long-standing objections of the educational-measurement specialists. At least in advanced-level courses, such tests remain one of the favorite forms of measurement for the very understandable reasons that they are an easy type of test to construct and appear to measure certain high-level abilities better than do the objective techniques.

The chief difficulties in using and assessing compositions as a measurement device are (1) eliciting the specific language items that the test writer particularly wishes to test and (2) finding a way to evaluate these free responses reliably and economically.

Composition tests will be treated at some length in our chapter on the testing of writing, and therefore a detailed discussion of the pros and cons will be deferred to that chapter. It should be stated at the outset, however, that in view of recent research it no longer appears necessary to adopt an either-or approach to the subject: there are unquestionably many language-testing situations in which the use of free-response techniques is highly inefficient, just as there is a narrow range of measurement objectives that may best be attained through the use of carefully prepared and scored compositions.

Scored Interview

Roughly parallel to the composition as a measure of students' written language is the scored interview as a device for assessing oral competence. Both are classed as free-response tests in which the subjects are allowed to express their answers in their own words in a relatively unstructured testing situation. The chief differences between these two devices, in addition to the obvious one that compositions call for writing and interviews call for speaking, are that in interviews (1) the examiner must provide a large number of cues throughout the performance and (2) the evaluation is generally made during the actual production of the responses, and there is no way for the examiner to reexamine the performance later in order to check the accuracy of his ratings.[2]

Most teachers who use the interview test do so not out of any strong conviction that it is the best of all possible techniques, but simply because they have no better way of assessing the oral competence of their students. Most of the weaknesses that we noted in our brief discussion of the composition apply to the interview as well. In our chapter on the testing of speaking, we shall deal at some length with this and alternative methods of measuring the oral abilities.

Multiple-choice Items

Multiple-choice or *selection* items types were developed to overcome a number of the weaknesses of the composition test that we noted earlier. Because of the highly structured nature of these items, the test writer can get directly at many of the specific skills and learnings he wishes to measure, and the examinee cannot evade difficult problems as he often can with compositions. As these items generally can be answered fairly rapidly, the test writer can include a large number of different tasks (that is, individual items) in the testing session. Finally, inasmuch as the examinee responds by choosing from several possible answers supplied by the test writer, scoring can be done quickly and involves no judgments as to degrees of correctness. Because of these virtues, multiple-choice tests tend to have superior *reliability* and *validity*, two important test characteristics which we shall examine in some detail in Chapter 2.

In its "classic" form, the multiple-choice item consists of (1) a *stem* or *lead*, which is either a direct question or an incomplete statement, and (2) two or more *choices* or *responses*, of which one is the *answer* and the others are *distracters*—that is, the incorrect responses.

```
      To walk through water is to _____

        A. wade        C. crouch
        B. scold       D. shrug
```

[2] An obvious exception is the interview that is tape-recorded. In most interview situations, however, the use of tapes is impracticable or undesirable because of its effect on the examinees.

The stem of this item is "To walk through water is to ———." The choices are the words marked A, B, C, D. The answer is choice A; the other choices are the distracters.

The very form of the multiple-choice item is the source of the most common objection to this testing method: the examinee does not have to think of his own answers; he "merely" makes choices. In our chapter on the testing of writing we shall treat this criticism in detail, citing a few of the many studies that give evidence that ability to *choose* the best of a number of given alternatives is actually quite highly related to ability to *compose* correct responses.

A more genuine disadvantage of multiple-choice tests is the very considerable skill and time that are required to prepare them. In deciding between compositions and selection methods, therefore, the classroom teacher must consider whether he wishes to put most of his effort into the preparation or into the scoring of his test. Fortunately, in many testing situations there is the possibility of another alternative—the short-answer test, which is a kind of compromise between the composition and selection types.

Short-answer Items

Short-answer tests combine some of the virtues of both multiple-choice and composition tests: the problems are short and highly structured, yet they provide the examinee with the opportunity to compose his own answers. As commonly used in language testing, short-answer items require the examinee either to complete a sentence or to compose one of his own according to very specific directions.

Directions--Complete each sentence by writing an appropriate form of the verb that is given in parentheses.

I wish I _____ (have) a new car.

Directions--Rewrite each statement to make it a negative question.

John knew the answer to the problem.

_____?

Short-answer items are extremely useful in informal classroom testing: they are relatively quick and easy to write and they require much less scoring time than would a composition. Their disadvantages for large-scale testing are, first, that they take longer to score than the multiple-choice types—an important factor when large numbers of papers are involved—and, second, that quite frequently there are a number of possible right answers, some of which the item writer might not even have considered at the time he prepared the test. Thus, in the first item given above, though the most likely completion would be "I wish I *had* a new car," we would have to accept *had had* as quite acceptable in certain contexts. And would such forms as *might have* and *could have had* be considered wrong? The problem of having to make such value judgments about the examinees' responses is avoided in the multiple-choice item types.

THE LANGUAGE SKILLS AND THEIR COMPONENTS

Language exists in two forms, the spoken and the written. Had we been treating this subject a generation ago, we would probably have put writing ahead of speaking. But the "new" language teaching methods introduced during and immediately following the Second World War have led us to change our order of priorities, and this present-day emphasis on the spoken form of the language is now reflected in our testing as well as our teaching of second languages.

Two linguistic activities are associated with both speech and writing: an encoding and a decoding process. *Speaking* and *writing* themselves are the encoding processes whereby we communicate our ideas, thoughts, or feelings through one or the other form of language; and *listening* and *reading* are the parallel decoding processes by which we "understand" either a spoken or a written message. We may therefore say that language includes four skills, or complexes of skills: listening, speaking, reading, and writing. It is perhaps in this order that we originally learned our native language, and it is in that order that foreign languages are now very frequently taught.

If we are correct in referring to the above as *complex* skills, what do we identify as the components of each? First of all, a moment's thought will establish two very important elements shared by all four skills: *grammatical structure* and *vocabulary*. In addition to these, skill in both auditory comprehension and oral production depends in part on mastery of the sound system of English. Thus we may list *phonology* as a third component of two of our four skills. And parallel to phonology in the spoken form of the language is *orthography* in the written form. For convenience we may wish to treat the sound and graphic systems together as an "either-or" component of our four skills. And finally, an aspect of listening, speaking, reading, and writing is the *rate and general fluency* with which these skills are performed. If, for example, a foreign student in this country cannot decode oral messages with reasonable speed and facility and can speak only in very halting fashion, he will find conversation with the native speaker of English virtually impossible. Likewise, if his reading rate is far below that of those who use English natively, he will be unable to keep up with his school assignments. And if his writing is slow and laborious, he will surely be handicapped in many school situations.

The four elements which we have now identified appear to constitute the principal linguistic components of the four skills, and any others we might think of (such as the ability to organize one's ideas in writing or to appreciate the style and tone of a reading selection) would probably prove either to be specialized applications of the four main components or else to be nonlinguistic in the strictest sense.[3]

Figure 1 illustrates the four components applied to the four language skills.[4] As will be seen from this chart, sixteen different combinations are possible. In practice, however, one can scarcely imagine a test which would attempt to adhere to such a detailed analysis. In testing (and in teaching, for that matter), the structures needed in listening and speaking would be regarded as the same, as generally would those of reading and writing. And while the test writer, like the teacher, would recognize the difference between active and passive vocabularies, it is likely that one vocabulary measure would suffice, though decisions would obviously have to be made about the balance between "use" and "recognition" items. We shall consider such matters in more detail in later chapters. Hopefully these remarks have, however, provided the rationale for our subsequent division of language tests into six types: listening, speaking, reading, and writing (the four skills); structure and vocabulary (two components which may merit separate testing by

---

[3]We shall return to these other abilities, however, in our chapters on the testing of the several language skills.

[4]The idea for this kind of breakdown of language skills was suggested by John B. Carroll, "Fundamental Considerations in Testing for English Language Proficiency of Foreign Students," *Testing the English Proficiency of Foreign Students*, Washington: Center for Applied Linguistics, 1961, pp. 31-40.

virtue of their general importance and applicability to all four skills areas).[5]

We shall return to our chart of skills and components later in the book when we are ready to discuss the important matter of test design. At that time we shall see how such a chart can serve as a checklist in the planning of a specific test.

Figure 1.   Chart of the Language Skills and Their Components

Components	Language Skills			
	Listening	Speaking	Reading	Writing
Phonology/ortho- graphy				
Structure				
Vocabulary				
Rate and general fluency				

CONTRASTIVE ANALYSIS AND LANGUAGE TESTING

One of the major principles in much modern second-language teaching is that a point-by-point comparison of target and background languages will provide the basis for more efficient instruction. Contrastive analysis is applied to every aspect of language: to phonology, morphology, syntax, and lexicon. It is even extended to cultural patterns that are thought to affect language learning and use. Through contrastive analysis we attempt to determine (1) what language patterns are identical in both languages, (2) what patterns in the target language have no near equivalents in the background language, and (3) what patterns in the background language have enough similarity to patterns in the target language (without being identical) to constitute major points of interference.

When one is designing a test of English for subjects who all share the same first language, contrastive analysis is undoubtedly useful in helping to estimate the probable relative difficulty of various patterns in the target language—in this case, English. Not to use

---

[5]This six-way division must be regarded as tentative, and quite possibly future research into language and language testing will establish a superior set of categories.

contrastive analysis in such situations would appear to be missing a rather good bet.

In many second-language testing situations, however, we are confronted by the practical need to prepare a "universal" test—one that can be used with students of disparate language backgrounds. In these situations, contrastive analysis can play little or no part. Unfortunately, some language teachers have become such avid proponents of the contrastive-analysis concept that they mistakenly condemn very good "universal" tests of English as a second language simply because they are not based on such an analysis. How, they ask, can one test effectively test everyone? Won't a "universal" test discriminate against students with some first languages while providing an unfair advantage to students with others? Most linguists who have acquired experience in language measurement would probably agree on the answer: if a test of English as a second language accurately samples a true cross section of the language, we need not be concerned that some students will find some problems easy that other students find difficult. In this regard, the test simply reflects the linguistic facts of life—that is, it mirrors the language-learning situation. The English vocabulary, for example, is in large part Latin-based, and therefore students from Romance-language countries may find ESL vocabulary tests easier than will, say, students whose other language is Arabic or Japanese. But unless we are prepared to say that it is "unfair" to expect the latter students to attain the same level of English proficiency as the former, we should not say that administering the same test to Spanish and French students that we give to Arabic and Japanese speakers is unfair.

There are, however, two aspects of test construction where "unfair practices" *are* liable to intrude. If the test maker's teaching experience has been largely confined to only one or two linguistic groups, he may tend quite unconsciously to generalize about English-learning difficulties on the basis of his limited experience and write items around the only problems he is familiar with. Or for his distracters he may concentrate on the specific "wrong" responses that are particularly common among speakers of one or two background languages. In such cases the test *will* be biased—and it requires a high degree of training and self-discipline for the test writer to overcome his own deficiencies.

Characteristics
of a Good Test

All good tests possess three qualities: *validity*, *reliability*, and *practicality*. That is to say, any test that we use must be *appropriate* in terms of our objectives, *dependable* in the evidence it provides, and *applicable* to our particular situation. To be sure, there are other test characteristics which are also of value, but these three constitute the *sine qua non*, without any one of which a test would be a poor investment in time and money. Whether the teacher is constructing his own test or is selecting a standard instrument for use in his class or school, he should certainly understand what these concepts mean and how to apply them.

Although most treatments of the subject put validity first, as being the most important of the three elements, we shall begin with reliability for the reason that it generally affects validity and that validity cannot be fully appreciated without a basic understanding of reliability.

RELIABILITY

The Meaning of Reliability

By reliability is meant the stability of test scores. A test cannot measure anything well unless it measures consistently. To have confidence in a measuring instrument, we would need to be assured, for example, that approximately the same results would be obtained (1) if we tested a group on Tuesday instead of Monday; (2) if we gave two parallel forms of the test to the same group on Monday *and* on Tuesday;[1] (3) if we scored a particular test on Tuesday instead of Monday; (4) if two or more competent scorers scored the test independently. It is clear from the foregoing that two somewhat different types of consistency or reliability are involved: reliability of the test itself, and reliability of the scoring of the test.

Test reliability is affected by a number of factors, chief among them being the adequacy of the sampling of tasks. Generally speaking, the more samples of students' performance we take, the more reliable will be our assessment of their knowledge and ability. It is this principle that in large part explains why the testing specialists have traditionally tended to favor objective examinations, in which a large number of items (individual measures) may be included in a testing session, rather than essay examinations, where the number of tasks must necessarily be quite limited. In addition, test reliability will be adversely affected if the conditions under which the test is administered tend to fluctuate from administration to administration. (The importance of maintaining uniform testing conditions will be considered in some detail in a later chapter.) Poor student motivation will also lower the reliability of a test. Sometimes the lack of proper motivation can be attributed to weaknesses in the test or the testing procedure (such as an examiner who introduces the test poorly), and sometimes it is caused by factors beyond either the test writer's or the examiner's control (e.g., by illness or personal problems affecting a number of the examinees). Such day-to-day fluctuations of test performance affect the *temporal stability* of the test.

---

[1]We should have to take into account, of course, a certain amount of score improvement resulting from the experience gained by the candidates through taking the first form of the test—the so-called "practice effect."

Scorer or *rater* reliability concerns the stability or consistency with which test performances are evaluated. Would one scorer give the same—or nearly the same—score repeatedly for the same test performance? Would two or more scorers assign equivalent scores for the same performance? Scorer reliability is nearly perfect in the case of multiple-choice tests (where the scorer is now very often a machine), but tends to be low in the case of free-response tests, like compositions, where a series of individual judgments must be made.

Types of Estimates of Reliability

Test reliability may be estimated in a number of ways. Obviously, the simplest technique would be to retest the same individuals with the same test. If the results of the two administrations were highly correlated, we could assume that the test had temporal stability—one of the concepts of reliability we discussed above. A moment's thought, however, will make evident the limitations of this method. If the time interval between the two testings is relatively short, the examinees' memories of their previous responses will make their two performances spuriously consistent and thus lead to an overestimate of test reliability. On the other hand, if the time interval is so long as to minimize the "memory factor," the examinees' proficiency may have undergone a genuine change, producing different responses to the same items, and thus the test reliability could be underestimated.[2]

A second method of computing reliability is with the use of alternate or parallel forms—that is, with different versions of the same test which are equivalent in length, difficulty, time limits, format, and all other such aspects. Where equivalent forms of a test exist, this method is probably the best, but even here practice effect, though reduced, will not be entirely eliminated.

A third method for estimating the reliability of a test consists in giving a single administration of one form of the test and then, by dividing the items into two halves (usually by separating odd-and even-numbered items), obtaining two scores for each individual. By such "split-half" procedures (of which the most common is by means of the Spearman-Brown formula), one obtains, in effect, two parallel

---

[2] In addition, the test-retest method would tell us nothing about the adequacy of our sample of items—whether another group of equivalent items measuring the same skills or learnings would produce about the same test results.

forms the results of which may be compared to provide a measure of the adequacy of the sampling.

Still another method often employed to determine test reliability is that of "rational equivalence" (the most familiar procedure being that developed by Kuder and Richardson). Here again, as in the case of "split-half" methods, reliability is estimated from a single administration of one form of the test. But in this case we are concerned with inter-item consistency as determined by the proportion of persons who pass and the proportion who do not pass each item.

Scorer reliability, as we have noted above, becomes a matter of great importance when the tests are of the free-response types. If test scoring is done by two or more raters, the reliability of their evaluations can easily be checked by comparing the scores they give for the same student responses. There are statistical techniques, too, for estimating the consistency with which one rater scores a free-response type, though a description of these would be beyond the scope of this book.

Estimating the Reliability of Speeded Tests

Speed tests are those in which the items are comparatively easy but the time limits are so short that few or none of the candidates can complete all items. Such tests are contrasted with *power* tests, in which item difficulty generally increases gradually but where ample time is given for all, or at least most, of the candidates to attempt every item.

Neither the "split-half" nor the "rational equivalence" technique of estimating reliability should be used with speed tests. Since there will be relatively few errors in such tests, an odd-even split, for instance, would yield a spuriously high correlation index—one close to "perfect," in fact. Test-retest or parallel forms are the methods best adapted to the measurement of speed-test reliability.

The Question of Satisfactory Reliability

A reliability quotient of 1.00 would indicate that a test is "perfectly" reliable. A quotient of zero would denote a complete absence of reliability. The coefficients found in actual practice usually fall somewhere between these two extremes. It is difficult to say precisely how high a reliability quotient should be before it may be regarded as satisfactory; much depends upon the kind of decisions one hopes to make on the basis of the test results. However, it would probably be safe to say that any standard test designed to make individual diagnoses (that is, to separate one examinee from another) should have a reliability quotient of at least .90, and preferably even somewhat higher.[3] Naturally, the reliability indices of "homemade" tests will tend to run somewhat lower—in the .70s or .80s, perhaps. Generally, reliability can be increased by lengthening the test, provided always that the additional material is similar in quality and difficulty to the original. But if satisfactory reliability could be obtained only by lengthening the test beyond all reasonable limits, it would obviously be wiser to revise the material or choose another test type.

The Standard Error of Measurement

As was suggested above, few if any forms of educational measurement are "perfectly" reliable. An *obtained score* on any test consists of the *"true" score* plus a certain amount of *test error*. This helps to explain why, for example, a student may score 60 on an English entrance test and 55 when later retested with an equivalent form of the test. The instructor or adviser who does not understand that test scores are simply estimates and that all educational measurement contains some degree of error is apt to ask why such an individual is "losing his English." The answer is that a decrease of 5 points is probably not statistically significant. The student does not, it is true, appear to have increased his English proficiency (providing always that the test is a good measurement of such proficiency and that the equivalent forms are really equivalent), but it would certainly be unsound to conclude that he is "going backward." Using the statistical estimate of reliability, test makers compute a further statistic known as the *standard error of measurement* (SE_{meas}) to estimate the limits within which an individual's obtained score on a test is likely to diverge from his true score.[4] If, for example, the

---

[3] Test reliability is commonly expressed in terms of a "correlation coefficient" whose statistical symbol is *r*. It must be understood that reliability quotients are not expressed as percents, even though figures like .85 and .92 have the appearance of percents.

[4] Both a shortcut method of estimating test reliability and the formula for estimating the standard error of measurement will be found in Chap. 12 of this book.

standard error of a given test is found to be 3 test-score units, we can say that the chances are 19 out of 20 that a subject's obtained score lies within 6 points (two standard errors of measurement), up or down, of the true figure.

Final Remarks about Reliability

Detailed information about the statistical techniques for estimating reliability can be found in the standard texts on educational measurement, a few of which are cited in the references at the back of this book. Our short discussion above was intended simply to explain what is meant by the term *reliability* and to suggest the importance of high reliability in the preparation or adoption of an educational measure. Whenever one is considering the adoption of a standard test, he should take into account the estimates of reliability which the publisher provides, and the nature of the groups on which these estimates are based. Likewise, when locally produced tests are to be used repeatedly to make important decisions about candidates, it is essential to obtain an estimate of the reliability of the instrument. On the other hand, for the usual classroom test, prepared by the class teacher and used but once, the computing of reliability coefficients is scarcely ever practicable. What is important for the classroom teacher, however, is to understand the chief factors affecting reliability and why and how some kinds of testing techniques are inherently more reliable than others. In our chapters on the testing of the various language skills, we shall make frequent references to the problems of obtaining satisfactory test and scorer reliability.

Finally, it must always be remembered that reliability refers purely and simply to the *precision* with which the test measures. No matter how high the reliability quotient, it is by no means a guarantee that the test measures what the test user *wants* to measure. Data concerning *what* the test measures must be sought from some source outside the statistics of the test itself. This problem will be considered in the following section.

VALIDITY

In the selection of any test, two questions must always be

considered: (1) *What* precisely does the test measure? and (2) *How well* does the test measure? If the test is found to be based upon a sound analysis of the skill or skills we wish to measure, and if there is sufficient evidence that test scores correlate fairly highly with actual ability in the skills area being tested, then we may feel reasonably safe in assuming that the test is valid for our purposes. A number of types of validation are applied to tests, all of them attempting to answer the above questions. In this brief survey we shall limit our consideration to just a few of the most common kinds.

Content Validity

If a test is designed to measure mastery of a specific skill or the content of a particular course of study, we should expect the test to be based upon a careful analysis of the skill or an outline of the course, and we should further expect the items to represent adequately each portion of the analysis or outline, not just those aspects which lend themselves most readily to a particular kind of test question.[5]

If, for example, a test is to measure foreign students' mastery of English sentence structure, an analysis must first be made of the language itself and decisions made on which matters need to be tested, and in what proportions. To the extent that the analysis accords with the views of recognized authorities in the skills area and the test then reflects such an analysis, it may be said to have *content validity*.

In choosing a test, therefore, we cannot simply accept the title which the authors have given it, for titles very often are misleading or inaccurate. We should expect the test makers to be able to provide us with information about the specific materials or skills being tested, and the basis for their selection.

Empirical Validity

The best way to check on the actual effectiveness of a test is to determine how test scores are related to some independent, outside criterion such as marks given at the end of a course or instructors' or

---

[5] The problems of deciding on test content will be discussed in succeeding chapters.

supervisors' ratings. If the evidence shows that there is a high correlation between test scores and a *trustworthy* external criterion, we are justified in putting our confidence in the *empirical validity* of the test.

Empirical validity is of two general kinds, *predictive* and *concurrent* (or *status*) validity, depending on whether test scores are correlated with subsequent or concurrent criterion measures. For example, if we use a test of English as a second language to screen university applicants and then correlate test scores with grades made at the end of the first semester, we are attempting to determine the predictive validity of the test. If, on the other hand, we follow up the test immediately by having an English teacher rate each student's English proficiency on the basis of his class performance during the first week and correlate the two measures, we are seeking to establish the concurrent validity of the test.

Publishers of standard tests should be expected to provide evidence of the validity of their measures. Estimates of test validity are usually expressed in terms of coefficients of correlation like those commonly used in estimating test reliability, with 1.00 as the highest possible index (indicating a perfect correlation between the two measures).[6] As with reliability, it is extremely difficult to say definitely how high a correlation must be to be judged satisfactory. Much will depend upon the nature of the external criterion. If the test is being correlated with another standard test of the same skill or skills (as when a short, simple test has been prepared to replace a longer and more complicated one), we should expect a fairly high correlation—one in the .70s or .80s, perhaps. On the other hand, when the external criterion is of a relatively subjective or inexact nature (supervisors' ratings or grades in a course, for example), we would not usually expect the coefficient to be much higher than the .50s. And of course the test we are validating may itself be a somewhat imprecise measure (e.g., a composition or scored interview), in which case the validity will be comparatively low. In short, *empirical validity depends in large part on the reliability of both test and criterion measure.*

---

[6] A simple rank-order method of correlation, which may be useful to teachers who wish to compare two test performances of small numbers of students, will be found in Chap. 12 of this book.

"Face Validity"

We conclude this brief survey of some common varieties of validation with what is most probably the most frequently employed type of all, *"face validity."* Here we mean simply the way the test *looks*—to the examinees, test administrators, educators, and the like. Obviously, this is not validity in the technical sense, and face validity can never be permitted to take the place of empirical validation or of the kind of authoritative analysis of content referred to above. Yet its importance should not be underestimated, for if the content of a test appears irrelevant, silly, or inappropriate, knowledgeable administrators will hesitate to adopt the test and examinees will lack the proper motivation.[7] Thus the test maker has an obligation always to keep face validity in mind, though sound methods of test construction should never be compromised merely to satisfy public opinion. Fortunately, it is quite possible to make tests that are technically sound and yet do not offend or insult those who take them.

PRACTICALITY

A third characteristic of a good test is its *practicality* or *usability*. A test may be a highly reliable and valid instrument but still be beyond our means or facilities. Thus in the preparation of a new test or the adoption of an existing one, we must keep in mind a number of very practical considerations.

Economy

As most educational administrators are very well aware, testing can be expensive. If a standard test is used, we must take into account the cost per copy, and whether or not the test books are reusable. Again, it should be determined whether several administrators and/or scorers will be needed, for the more personnel who must be involved in giving and scoring a test, the more costly the process becomes.

[7]An example might be an English reading comprehension test designed for American children which is given to adult foreign learners of English just because the two groups are thought to have a similar degree of proficiency in the language.

Closely related to economy in dollars is economy in time. In writing or selecting a test, we should certainly pay some attention to how long the administering and scoring of it will take. Yet in choosing a short test rather than a longer one, we must proceed with caution. As we observed earlier in this chapter, both reliability and validity depend in large part on the adequacy of our sampling and the breadth of our appraisal. Our task, then, is to select an instrument which is of sufficient length to yield dependable and meaningful results but which will also fit comfortably into the time that can be made available for testing. This point is of particular importance when the test must be administered in the classroom and scored by the classroom teacher.

Ease of Administration and Scoring

Other considerations of test usability involve the ease with which the test can be administered. Are full, clear directions provided so that the test administrator can perform his tasks quickly and efficiently? Does the test call for elaborate mechanical devices (such as audio equipment) that may not be readily accessible or cannot easily be installed in the rooms available?[8] Must each test be administered separately, thereby greatly complicating the testing process?

Scoring procedures, too, can have a significant effect on the practicality of a given instrument. Particularly when large numbers of examinees are involved, we need to know whether the test must be scored subjectively or is objective in nature. If the latter, we may wish to determine whether a standard answer sheet is used, so that the papers may be run through a machine. Indeed, a separate answer sheet will also facilitate hand scoring of the tests, for the scoring of responses made directly in a test book is extremely laborious.

Ease of Interpretation

If a standard test is being adopted, it is important that we

---

[8] Fortunately, most of the established language tests require no more equipment than a tape recorder or record player, if even that, and so the problem of mechanical aids has not generally been a serious one—except, perhaps, in some overseas situations. However, some of the new oral-production tests require that each examinee record his responses, and some recent experimental language-aptitude measures call for filmstrip projectors; clearly these will affect the usability of the instruments in some situations.

examine and take into account the data which the publisher provides. Is there an up-to-date test manual that gives clear information about test reliability and validity and about norms for appropriate reference groups? If we plan to use the test over a long period of time, we shall almost certainly wish to develop local norms of our own. However, we need to have some general guidance as to the meaning of test scores to begin with, for without this it is extremely difficult to use an instrument in an efficient manner.[9]

---

[9]Detailed interpretive data are seldom available for very new tests. The responsible test publisher will, however, provide tentative data from the outset and will supplement and update these at frequent intervals.

Testing Grammatical Structure

GENERAL NATURE OF THE ESL STRUCTURE TEST

There is an essential difference between the traditional "grammar" test for the native speaker of English and the kind of structure test appropriate for the foreign learner. Inasmuch as it can generally be assumed that the native speaker of the language has mastered a grammatical system largely or wholly acceptable for informal discourse,[1] "grammar" tests at least on the high school and college levels have usually concentrated on matters of style and diction appropriate for rather formal written English. On the other hand, structure tests for foreign students will have as their purpose the testing of control of the basic grammatical patterns of the spoken language. Such tests would constitute no challenge for native speakers of standard English, who, except for carelessness, would be expected to make perfect scores. Only for the most advanced foreign learners are tests of formal style and diction at all meaningful, and

---

[1] Obvious exceptions are those children now termed culturally or educationally "disadvantaged," whose need for special language instruction and measurement we are at last beginning to recognize and act upon.

then they are better treated as tests of writing ability and kept quite separate from the tests of structure we are discussing in this chapter.[2]

DETERMINATION OF TEST CONTENT

The preparation of a structure test should always begin with the setting up of a detailed outline of the proposed test content. The outline should specify not only which structures are to be tested, but the percentage of items to be written around each problem. This outline may have to be modified somewhat on the basis of the results of pretesting,[3] but great care must be taken to ensure that the final form of the test includes *a broad range of relevant grammatical problems in proportions which reflect their relative importance.* This point cannot be emphasized too strongly, for there is a common tendency in grammar testing to end up with a disproportionate number of items testing a few structural points that happen to be the easiest to put into the test writer's favorite item format. Clearly, a test constructed with such a bias cannot serve as a fair or valid measure of either a student's general progress or his overall competence in the language.

Selection of the structures to be included in an achievement test is relatively easy, inasmuch as the class text can and should be used as the basis for our test. As a rule, the test should include the full range of structures that were taught in the course, and each structural type should receive about the same emphasis in the test that it received in the classroom.[4]

In general proficiency testing, on the other hand, the choice of structures is a rather difficult one which to some extent must be made subjectively. Perhaps the best approach is to examine a number of standard texts prepared for students at the level of the intended test population, listing the structures commonly presented in these works and noting the emphasis which each receives. Of course if the test

---

[2] Tests of writing will be treated in Chap. 7.

[3] Pretesting involves trying out the test materials on a group similar to that for whom the test is being designed. Pretesting procedures will be discussed in Chap. 9.

[4] This should at least be the initial working plan. However, pretesting may show that some structural points have been so thoroughly mastered by the population that there is little or no value in including them in the final form of the test.

writer is himself a teacher of English as a second language, he will wish to use his own judgment in determining the weight to be given to the various grammatical points.

ITEM TYPES

1. Completion (multiple-choice). The most common type of multiple-choice structure item presents a context in which one or more words are missing, followed by several alternative completions. The following examples illustrate three versions of this basic type.

```
Mary (lives) (is living) (has lived) in New York since 1960.
        A        B           C
Mary _____ in New York since 1960.
  A. lives                 C. has lived
  B. is living


"Is Mary Baker still in Chicago?" "No; _____ in New York since 1960."
  A. she lives              C. she's living
  B. she'd lived            D. she's lived
```

All three styles have been used many times, and apparently with about equal success, and preference for one over another seems to be largely a matter of personal choice. In terms of space, version 1 is certainly the most economical. Version 2 is felt by some to be less confusing to the examinees because it does not interrupt the context with the alternatives, though there appears to be no real evidence that examinees perform more effectively when the items have this form. Version 3 is favored by many language teachers and specialists because the dialogue form provides more context and therefore may make the problem somewhat clearer. There is undoubtedly some merit in this argument; moreover, some structural problems seem to require more setting than one short sentence, and therefore the dialogue format may actually allow more flexibility in the selection of test problems.

2. Sentence alternatives (multiple-choice). Another item type does away with the item stem altogether and simply presents several sentences from which the examinee chooses the acceptable version.

```
A. Mary is living in New York since 1960.
B. Mary lives in New York since 1960.
C. Mary has lived in New York since 1960.
```

Some test writers and users have expressed a preference for this item type over the preceding on the grounds that it is less confusing for the examinee to work with complete sentences. Again, however, there appears to be no strong evidence that students do, indeed, perform better on this item type.

3. Sentence interpretation (multiple-choice). A third type of structure item presents a stimulus and then asks for an interpretation. This becomes a kind of reading comprehension task in which the crucial clues are structural.

```
"An old friend of John's family brought him news of his uncle last night."
Him refers to

A. an old friend          C. the uncle
B. John
```

If, as some believe, it is important to separate comprehension from production in tests of structure, this item type may have something to commend it, at least in tests for elementary-level learners. More advanced students, however, will find such items extremely easy unless the test writer resorts to very complicated contexts that one would rarely if ever encounter in daily speech.[5] Moreover, it is quite difficult to frame normal sentences that will yield three or four attractive, well-expressed choices of interpretation.

4. Scrambled sentence (multiple-choice). For the testing of word order, test writers sometimes use the device of the scrambled sentence in which the examinee rearranges a jumbled series of elements so as to form an acceptable sentence.

[5]The following is a close imitation of some of the items that have occurred in sentence-interpretation tests.

```
"The friend of the doctor that Charles met when he visited his daughter
and her husband came to the library today."
The person who visited the library was

A. the friend           D. the daughter
B. the doctor           E. the daughter's husband
C. Charles
```

Sometimes, too, the test writer will deliberately omit punctuation which would provide an obvious clue to meaning:

```
When _____ ?
    A. plan           C. to go
    B. do             D. you
```

As a classroom exercise or informal test on an elementary level, this device probably has some merit, younger students in particular being intrigued by its puzzle-solving aspects. On a more advanced level, however, this item type has several drawbacks. First, it is extremely difficult to compose items of just the right level of difficulty: the problems tend to be very easy unless the sentences are made rather long and complex, in which event the task may become more a test of intelligence than of simple structural control. Secondly, with all but the simplest sentences it is hard to avoid scrambled word groups that cannot be assembled in a variety of acceptable ways, making the scoring time-consuming when large numbers of papers are involved. And in multiple-choice testing there is the problem of devising a clear and simple way for answers to be recorded on the answer sheet and to be scored. But more important than any of the above, it seems doubtful whether anything is really accomplished by the scrambled-sentence technique that cannot be more effectively and economically achieved by other methods.[6]

```
"Have your friend come with you"  The speaker is

    A. making an observation     C. extending an invitation
    B. asking a question
```

Inasmuch as we teach our students to be sensitive to punctuation as an important signaling device of the written language, its omission in testing creates a highly artificial situation which would appear neither necessary nor, indeed, desirable.

[6]For instance, in the above example we are testing the word-order pattern in questions beginning with question words. The same pattern can easily be tested by other selection item types:

```
When _____ to go to New York?
    A. you are planning      C. you do plan
    B. you plan              D. do you plan
```

(Note, by the way, that the construction "When you plan to go?"—so natural to many foreign learners of English—is not possible in the scrambled item, where all the jumbled words must be utilized in the rearrangement.)

5. Completion (supply type). Returning to type 1, we may use the completion item type as a fill-in exercise.

> <u>Directions</u>--Complete the sentences by writing a form of the verb given
> in parentheses.
> Mary _____ (live) in New York since 1960.
>
> <u>Directions</u>--Complete the sentences by using the prepositions <u>before</u>,
> <u>during</u>, <u>since</u>.
> Mary has been living in New York _____ 1960.

This item type is extremely useful in informal classroom-testing situations. Such items are much easier to prepare than the multiple-choice types, and they require a certain amount of composition on the part of the students. Their disadvantages for large-scale testing are the same as with all supply types: they are much more time-consuming to score than multiple-choice items, and there may be several possible correct answers to some of the items so that different scorers might judge the same response differently.

6. Conversion (supply type). Another popular type of short-answer structure test requires the examinees to convert or transform a series of sentences in a specified manner—by changing them from present to past tense, from active to passive voice, from singular to plural, and so forth. The comments given above for item type 5 may be applied to the conversion type as well.

ADVICE ON ITEM WRITING

Inasmuch as the completion item types are the most common ways of testing structure objectively, we shall concentrate our attention on the problems of writing these items, using the dialogue form for our examples. Most of the principles which apply to the preparation of these items are appropriate for other multiple-choice item types as well.

1. The language of the dialogues should read like spoken English. Common contractions should be employed wherever they would normally occur in speech. Avoid constructions usually found only in formal writing.

Bad item   "John got a very poor grade on the test."

               " _____, this would not have happened."

               A. He had studied
               B. Had he studied
               C. He studied
               D. He **was** studying

As it stands, this item would be too formal for a test of spoken English. Changed as follows, it would be acceptable:

    "John got a very poor grade on the test."
    "Yes, but that wouldn't have happened if_____."
     A. he'd studied
     B. he's studying
     C. he studies
     D. he'll study

2. The second part of the dialogue should sound like a natural response to the first part. Avoid responses that sound like artificial classroom drills.

Bad item

"Can the girls read French?" "No, Mary can't read French and_____."

   A. neither can Jane
   B. Jane either can't
   C. so can't Jane
   D. Jane can't, too

The above response to the question would be highly unlikely in normal conversation. The item could be rewritten as follows:

        "Mary can't read French."
        "And _____."

         A. neither can Jane
         B. Jane either can't
         C. so can't Jane
         D. Jane can't, too

3. All distracters should be definitely *non-English*; care must therefore be taken not to present regional or social variants of

English as "wrong" answers.[7] To help ensure that his distracters do not contain forms acceptable in another English dialect, the test writer should ask other native speakers of English to review his items.

Bad item

```
"The maid is coming today."
"Please have her _____ the windows in my room."
     A. to wash
     B. washing
     C. to washing
     D. wash
```

Many native English speakers would have no objection to A, "Please have her to wash the windows." It should therefore be replaced with a form which all native English speakers would reject, such as *washed*.

4. No distracters should include "errors" which would appear in writing but not in speech.

Bad item

```
"Do you drink coffee?"
"Not any more, but I _____."
     A. used to
     B. am used to
     C. use to
     D. used to do
```

As normally spoken, both A and C would be pronounced alike. The choice of the correct answer, then, becomes a spelling problem and as such has no place in a test designed to measure control of the structures of conversational English. The above item could be salvaged by changing choice C to "used to drink." Another example would be the form "10-cents stamps," which in speech could not generally be distinguished from the "correct" form, "10-cent stamps." The same problem could be tested safely with a phrase like "2-dollar(s) pipe."

---

[7] Although there is some disagreement on the point, it would seem generally advisable not to use substandard English ("he don't," "it wasn't hardly," "they done it") in the distracters of a structure test for foreign students. The emphasis should be on clear-cut contrasts between English and non-English in the strictest sense; the foreign learner should not be required to make judgments on levels of usage. In like manner the distinctions between such verb pairs as *sit/set, lie/lay, rise/raise* (which many native speakers of English do not make) should be considered to lie outside the province of the structure test. (They might, however, be considered for inclusion in an advanced-level test of *writing ability*. See Chap. 7.)

4 Testing Auditory Discrimination and Comprehension

TESTS OF SOUND DISCRIMINATION

One of the early steps in much modern language instruction is to teach the learner to discriminate between phonetically similar but phonemically separate sounds in the target language. Quite often this instruction includes drill with *minimal pairs*—sets of words which differ from each other in just one phonemic contrast. Thus, for example, a teacher working with the important English distinction between /i/ and /I/ might write two columns of words on the board, such as:

sleep	slip
team	Tim
steel	still
deep	dip
reach	rich

and then, as recognition drill, pronounce words randomly from the two columns, asking the members of the class to identify the column from which each word is taken. Such an exercise is, in reality, a two-choice "objective test," and most sound discrimination tests are simply variations and expansions of this common classroom technique.

Item Types

1. Word sets in isolation. In the simplest form of objective sound discrimination test, the examiner pronounces pairs of words and asks the examinees to indicate whether the two words in each pair are the same or are different.

The examinee hears:

On his answer sheet the examinee circles *S* for *same* or *D* for *different:*

```
1. "cot - caught"          1.  S  Ⓓ
2. "ship - sheep"          2.  S  Ⓓ
3. "law - law"             3.  Ⓢ  D
```

Because of its simplicity, this item type can be used effectively at even the earliest stages of language learning. It does have, however, a weakness shared by all two-choice item types: examinees have a 50 percent probability of answering the problems correctly just by pure chance. To lessen the effects of guessing, we can use word triplets, the examinees being asked to indicate which two words in each set are the same.

The examinee hears:

On his answer sheet the examinee indicates which two words are the same:

```
1. "cot - caught - cot"      1.  ①  2  ③
2. "law - law - low"         2.  ①  ②  3
3. "sheep - ship - ship"     3.  1  ②  ③
```

With three possible answers, word-triplet items would generally be preferable to word pairs in a formal testing situation.[1]

2. Words in context. The next step is to insert the minimal pair problems into complete sentences, that is, to use sentences which might be misunderstood because of the examinees' failure to perceive one phonemic contrast. Sometimes these tests make use of pictures.[2]

---

[1]When reading word sets, the examiner must take care to use the same falling intonation pattern throughout: cŏt căught cŏt.

[2]The problems of using picture alternatives will be discussed under "Tests of Auditory Comprehension" below.

The examinee hears: "It was a very large ship."
The examinee indicates which picture in his test book
illustrates the spoken sentence:

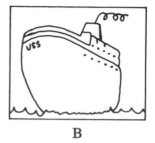

A   B

On an intermediate level where students can be expected to read
simple sentences, the choices can be given in writing:

The examinee hears:	The examinee reads in his test book:	The examinee marks his answer sheet:
1. "It was a very large ship."	1. It was a very large (A) ship (boat) (B) sheep (animal)	1. Ⓐ B

Note that in the above item the test words given in the test book
have been followed by simple synonyms: *boat* after *ship*, *animal*
after *sheep*. The purpose of the synonyms is to prevent the examinee
from checking the wrong response simply through a spelling error.

Much more could certainly be written about sound discrimination testing, but the foregoing examples illustrate some of the
most common item types and should suggest both the strengths and
limitations of these devices. Sound discrimination tests are very
useful on the beginning and intermediate levels of instruction,
particularly as measures of achievement in courses which emphasize
drill on phonemic distinctions. On the high-intermediate and
advanced levels we are more concerned with measuring general
comprehension of complete utterances and sequences of utterances,
a complex of skills in which ability to perceive minimal sound
contrasts plays only a small part. The remainder of this chapter will
be devoted to a consideration of such tests.

TESTS OF AUDITORY COMPREHENSION

General Nature of the Tests

In foreign-language testing, auditory comprehension tests are designed to measure the accuracy with which the subjects are able to decode samples of speech in the target language. These samples may be one-sentence requests, questions, or statements of fact; they may be brief, simulated conversations; or they may be extended stretches of expository discourse. But whatever the nature of the samples, the subjects will be required to deal simultaneously with a variety of phonological, grammatical, and lexical "signals," and by their responses to reveal how well they can derive meaning from these signaling elements of the language when used for verbal communication.

Use of Recordings versus a Live Voice

In the preparation of formal tests of auditory comprehension, the test maker must decide whether the utterances will be put on tape or records or be delivered "live" by the examiner.

The use of mechanical devices always involves extra preparation and labor, and in some places the equipment may be difficult to acquire and/or install in the testing area. Moreover, if the recording and the playing mechanisms are not both of very high quality, test performance will be adversely affected. On the other hand, the use of good sound equipment is the best guarantee of high test reliability, for the verbal stimuli will then be uniformly presented, and the performance of one group of examinees can confidently be compared with that of another. And in foreign countries where native speakers of the test language are not available as examiners, the use of recordings becomes the only acceptable method of administering an aural test.

Professional testing organizations often provide both recordings and scripts with their auditory comprehension tests, urging the use of the former whenever possible but allowing a "live" reading when it is the only way the test can be administered. If answer sheets are then returned to the central organization for scoring, a report must be submitted by the local examiner describing the equipment that was used or indicating that the test was delivered "live." In the interpretation and use of test results, account can then be taken of the conditions under which the administration was carried out.

Item Types

1. **Directions requiring action responses.** In the testing of young children, an effective test can be constructed using a series of oral directions or instructions eliciting simple action responses.

1. Please bring me the green book.
2. Please open the window just a little bit.
3. Please turn the light on and then turn it off again.

The advantages of this type of test are, first, that it does not require responses which involve another language skill such as reading or speaking, and, second, that the simple listen-and-do formula is one that is easily understood by children and does not call for elaborate general explanations or the manipulation of the usual testing apparatus of pencils and test booklets. Its chief limitation is that the test utterances will naturally be confined to one general grammatical type, the imperative or request construction. It will generally be advisable, therefore, to combine direction items with at least one other auditory comprehension type. Fortunately, some of the other devices described below can be adapted to the testing of young children, and attention will be drawn to such possibilities.

2. **Questions and statements (multiple-choice).** For examinees who are able to read easy English sentences, an effective and relatively uncomplicated comprehension test can be constructed using verbal stimuli and printed alternatives. The stimuli consist of short questions and statements which the candidate hears (once) but cannot see. The *question* items are to be answered by the selection of the one logical answer from among several printed in the test booklet. The *statements* are answered by the selection of the one printed alternative which accurately paraphrases the statement heard. The following examples illustrate the question and statement forms.[3]

---

[3]The examples in this and the following section are taken from the Handbook for Candidates prepared for *TOEFL* (*Test of English as a Foreign Language*). They are reprinted by permission of Educational Testing Service and the College Entrance Examination Board. Copyright © 1967 by Educational Testing Service. All rights reserved.

Question item

The examinee hears: The examinee reads:

"When did Tom come here?"   A. By train.
                                                    B. Yes, he did.
                                                    C. To study history.
                                                    D. Last night.

Statement item

The examinee hears: "John dropped the letter in the mailbox."
The examinee reads:

A. John sent the letter.
B. John opened the letter.
C. John lost the letter.
D. John destroyed the letter.

By means of such items, a wide range of sentence types may be tested within a short space of time, and there is evidence that even a short test of this nature is both a reliable and a valid measure of general comprehension.[4]

The chief disadvantage of this test type is that the alternatives are printed, so that auditory comprehension is in part tested through the medium of reading. The reading factor can, however, be minimized if care is taken to keep the printed choices brief and grammatically and lexically simple, and by allowing enough time for examinees to read the alternatives at a relatively easy pace.[5]

To eliminate reading altogether, some auditory comprehension tests use a set of pictures for the choices.

The examinee hears: "John's house is the one with the two big trees on either side."

---

[4]For example, the 40-item *Listening Test* developed by the American Language Institute of Georgetown University has a test reliability of .92, and test performance has been found to correlate about .71 with teachers' general ratings of their students' auditory comprehension ability.
[5]Twelve seconds appears to be a reasonable interval for the answering of these items.

The examinee indicates which picture in his test book illustrates the spoken sentence:

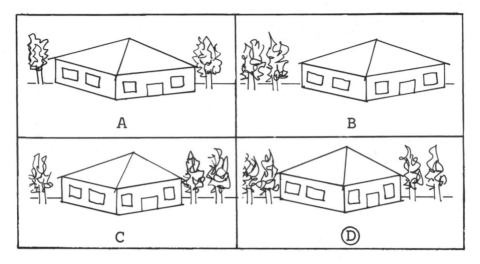

The complete absence of writing greatly commends the use of picture items in tests of aural comprehension, and a number of fairly effective tests of this kind have been developed. There are, however, certain serious problems that seem intrinsically connected with the construction and application of these devices.

First and foremost, unless the problems are on the easy side, they tend to be extremely difficult to illustrate simply and unambiguously. Distracters that are close enough to the right pictorial "answer" to be at all attractive are apt to be defensible as correct choices themselves. Informal experiments have shown that even native speakers of English have trouble with some of the problems in the published tests for foreign students.[6] The difficulties for foreign students, particularly those from non-Western countries, are further compounded by the occasional use of special pictorial conventions

[6]Particularly questionable are the items which attempt to deal with verb tense by illustrating several steps in an action. For example, to accompany the stimulus

"Where is the book?"
"Mary put it on the desk."

the test writer might use three pictures showing (A) a woman bringing a book to a desk; (B) the woman placing the book on the desk; (C) the woman walking away from the book on the desk. It would seem to be all a matter of one's own point of view whether (A), (B), or (C) is judged the best depiction of the stimulus.

that may not be as familiar in their cultures as in ours. One wonders, for example, about the universality of the pictorial conventions shown in the following pictures—all of them devices which appear in published auditory comprehension tests for foreign students:

"He's been work-ing *very hard*."	"She brought a cup of *hot* coffee."
"He *looked* the people *over*."	"The light was *on* when we left."

As a result of these difficulties, most of the existing picture tests of auditory comprehension fall into three categories:

1. Those that are really too easy for use beyond the elementary level

2. Those that are difficult but for the wrong reasons (inclusion of ambiguous and/or "culturally loaded" items)

3. Those that are too heavily weighted with just one or two kinds of problems (often those concerning spatial relationships)

Secondly, it appears entirely possible that, whatever the intrinsic merit of a picture test, it will appear rather silly and childish to some adult examinees, an attitude that could conceivably affect the reliability and validity of the measure.

Finally, picture tests of professional quality are very expensive and time-consuming to prepare, though it would be wrong to discard a measurement device on this basis alone.

The foregoing paragraphs are not intended to dissuade the test writer from any experimentation with the use of pictures in auditory comprehension testing, but simply to warn of some inherent dangers and to explain why some test makers have shown a preference for other item types—which, of course, have their own problems and shortcomings. Particularly in the testing of pre-literate children, the use of picture tests may be unavoidable.

3. Dialogues (multiple-choice). Another type of auditory test item using oral stimuli and printed alternatives consists of a brief dialogue followed by a comprehension question asked in a third voice. The question is answered by the selection of the correct answer from among several printed in the test booklet.

The examinee hears:	The examinee reads:
(man) "Hello, Mary. This is Mr. Smith at the office. Is Bill feeling any better today?"	A. At the office.
	B. On his way to work.
	C. Home in bed.
	D. Away on vacation.
(woman) "Oh, yes, Mr. Smith. He's feeling much better now. But the doctor says he'll have to stay in bed until Monday."	

(third voice) "Where is Bill now?"

Because of the greater context which it provides, the dialogue item type is favored by some test writers over the statement-in-isolation type previously described. It is felt that the dialogue is both fairer and more realistic as a test of general comprehension. Moreover, it is undoubtedly appropriate to test understanding of the relationship between two utterances or sets of utterances. Although it might be argued that the dialogue requires the examinee to hold a good deal more data in his head, in actual fact the additional context tends to make these items somewhat easier, on the whole, than the isolated statements. A further advantage is that the dialogue makes it easier to test the kind of colloquial language that abounds in casual conversation and may even be used to measure understanding of that vital but elusive quality known as "tone of voice," as will be illustrated at the end of this chapter.

4. Lectures (multiple-choice). Advanced-level auditory comprehension tests have also been devised to test college applicants' ability to follow classroom lectures delivered in the applicants' second language. The value of such a measurement is obvious: foreign students who enroll in an institution where English is the medium of instruction will begin with a serious handicap if they cannot comprehend, and keep up with, lectures delivered in the more formal style of the academic lecturer and characterized by long stretches of uninterrupted discourse crammed with significant data. The lecture test attempts to reproduce as realistically as possible the typical lecture situation.

Directions to Examinees:

In [this part of the test] you will hear about eight minutes of a university lecture. As you listen, you should take notes on important facts and dates which you might not otherwise remember. A page is provided for your notes in your test book. At the end of the test you must hand in this page with the rest of your test book. However, the notes are for your use only, and they will not be graded.

After you have listened to this brief lecture, you will answer a series of questions about what you have heard. In deciding on an answer, you may, of course, consult your notes. However, do not try to answer any of the questions while the lecture is being presented. If you do, you may not be able to answer some of the questions because you have missed some important points.[7]

At the conclusion of the recorded lecture, the examinees are directed to turn again to their test books and answer a series of multiple-choice questions about the content of the lecture. The examinees can answer these questions at their own speed, referring to their notes as needed.

Great care must be taken in the preparation of the test lecture. The subject must be a fairly general one that will not favor some examinees and discriminate against others by virtue of their previous training and experience. (For example, a lecture on the technical problems of interplanetary travel might be relatively easy for some science students while being largely unintelligible to literature majors.) At the same time, the use of subjects more or less in the

[7] These directions have been taken from the Handbook for Candidates prepared for TOEFL and are reprinted by permission of Educational Testing Service and the College Entrance Examination Board. Copyright © 1967 by Educational Testing Service. All rights reserved.

"public domain" (such as the landing of the Pilgrims) must be avoided, inasmuch as some students may already be quite familiar with the material. Perhaps the best solutions are to base the lecture on a little-known aspect of a familiar subject or to *invent* a person or event, in which case the examinees should be informed of the fictitious nature of the material.

Lecture tests are obviously suitable only for very mature and advanced students of English. There is no reason, however, why the same general format cannot be used in testing auditory comprehension on the lower levels. Children, for example, might be told a short, simple story, to be followed up with oral questions and answers.

> Right after breakfast, John went to the post office because he had an important letter to mail. When he got there, he found that the doors were locked. He'd forgotten that it was a holiday, and so the post office was closed.
> 1. When did John go to the post office?
> 2. Why did he go there?
> 3. Why were the doors locked?

Suggestions for Writing Items

Several general principles may be applied to the writing of most types of auditory comprehension items.

1. Both the stimulus and the item choices should sound as much as possible like informal, spoken English (except, of course, in the simulated lectures). Where, for instance, elliptical constructions and sentence fragments would be normal in conversation (as in the response utterances in dialogues or in the choices that accompany question items), they should be used.

2. The oral stimulus should include only high-frequency lexical items. We are concerned in auditory comprehension tests with the understanding of whole utterances and sequences of utterances; low-frequency vocabulary should be tested separately in tests designed specifically for that purpose.

3. To minimize the reading factor, printed answer choices should be brief (preferably five to six words, not as a rule over eight to ten) and lexically and grammatically simple.

4. When, as in dialogues, a *sequence* of utterances is being tested, the problem should hinge on an understanding of the relationship of the utterances to one another. To put it another way, each utterance in a sequence should have some specific function in terms of the test problem. No portion of the stimulus should be used merely to confuse the listener or to divert his attention from the point that is to be tested.[8]

The following examples of question, statement, and dialogue items will illustrate the foregoing principles and suggest something of the range of problem types that can be tested.

1. **Questions.** Question items should test comprehension of a wide variety of interrogative types: those beginning with *be* and *do* forms, with modals, and with question words. The distracters should be natural-sounding responses that might be made by a listener who picked up the wrong question signal.

Example A   "Is John a teacher like his father?"

  A. No, the teacher doesn't like him.
  B. Yes, his father is a teacher.
  C. No, John is a doctor.
  D. Yes, John likes him very much.

In the stimulus, *like* may be taken to mean "be fond of"; hence choices A and D. And there may appear to the less proficient listener to be three people involved here: John, the teacher, and the father. This possible misinterpretation is reflected in choice A. Choice B assumes that some listeners may misunderstand the question as primarily concerning John's father. In the responses, note the balance of two affirmatives and two negatives.

Example B   "Do you know where Mary's brother is now?"

  A. Yes, I've known him for years.
  B. She's in Chicago.
  C. Yes, I know her very well.
  D. He's in New York.

---

[8] Items such as the following are sometimes found in tests of auditory comprehension. Note how little of the stimulus has any relevance to the test question.

"There are 30 children in John's class. Their teacher is a young woman whose name is Miss Jones. All the children like her very much. *How many children are there in the class?*"

This rather easy item assumes three possible misunderstandings of the stimulus: "Do you know Mary?" "Do you know Mary's brother?" "Do you know where Mary is now?" A partial comprehension of the stimulus might lead to any of these interpretations.

Example C   "Must I wear my coat when we go to the restaurant tonight?"

A. I don't know where.
B. At eight o'clock.
C. Yes, we'll go tonight.
D. I really think you should.

The distracters assume that the poor listener will react to one or another segment of the test utterance and will interpret the question as "Where is my coat?" "When do we go?" or "Do we go to the restaurant tonight?" Note that choice B is a sentence fragment and choices A and D are somewhat elliptical, as they would tend to be in conversation.

Example D   "How much time will you have to spend in New York?"

A. About a hundred dollars.
B. Yes, I'll have the time.
C. Just two days.
D. Yes, I must.

The less proficient examinee may respond to several wrong signals in the stimulus. "How much . . . will you have to spend" may seem to concern money; "will you have [time]" seems to require a yes/no answer; "will you have to" may sound like a question concerning necessity.

2. **Statements.** A wide variety of problem types can and should be included in a statement-comprehension test. The following examples illustrate just a few of the common categories.

Example A: Comparison

"Now that I'm in college, I prefer history to science."

A. I like science better than history.
B. I like neither history nor science.
C. I like history better than science.
D. I like science just as much as history.

Example B: Time

"John's plane was due to arrive at noon, but it was half an hour late."

A. The plane arrived at eleven-thirty (11:30).
B. The plane arrived at twelve o'clock (12:00).
C. The plane arrived at twelve-thirty (12:30).
D. The plane arrived at one o'clock (1:00).

Example C: Number

"There were forty seats in the bus, but only half of them were taken."

A. There were 20 passengers.
B. There were 30 passengers.
C. There were 50 passengers.
D. There were 60 passengers.

Example D: Condition

"I'm sure Bill would have returned the book if he'd known Mary really needed it."

A. Bill knew Mary needed the book.
B. Bill didn't return the book.
C. Mary didn't really need the book.
D. I'm sure Bill returned the book.

Example E: Noun compound

"I'm sorry, but I asked for a butter knife, not a soup spoon."
A. I asked for some butter.
B. I asked for a spoon.
C. I asked for some soup.
D. I asked for a knife.

Example F: Negative

"Bill declined Jack's offer of money."

A. Bill wouldn't accept Jack's money.
B. Bill wouldn't give Jack money.
C. Jack wouldn't offer Bill any money.
D. Jack wouldn't take Bill's money.

3. Dialogues. Though they may cover an extremely wide range of subject matter, dialogue items are essentially of two general types: (*a*) those which test comprehension and recall of the explicit information given by the speakers, and (*b*) those which test the examinee's ability to draw inferences and conclusions from the oral exchange. A comprehensive dialogue test should include items of both varieties.

The following is an example of an item which aims simply at testing *understanding of the surface meaning* of the dialogue.

Example A

"I saw George Brown today, but I forgot to ask him what his brother's doing now."

"Oh, I can tell you that. He's working in a bank to save enough money to go back to college."

(third voice) "What news did the man hear from the woman?"

A. That George has gone back to college.
B. That George's brother is working in a bank.
C. That George's brother has gone back to college.
D. That George is working in a bank.

Note than an understanding of both utterances is necessary for the answering of this item: the first utterance establishes that it is George's *brother* who is the center of interest, and the second utterance tells us what he (the brother) is doing now.

In contrast to the above, the following items all call for some degree of *interpretation* of what the two speakers say.

Example B

(man) "This has been the wettest April I can remember. I've almost forgotten what the sun looks like."

(woman) "Yes, and it certainly would be nice to be able to put these heavy clothes away for a while."

(third voice) "What kind of weather have these people apparently been having?"

A. Hot and dry
B. Cold and rainy
C. Cold and dry
D. Hot and rainy

Although the above item is a fairly easy one, it illustrates how the solution can be made to depend on implicit, rather than explicit, information. In general, the more indirectly the crucial information is given, the more difficult the item will be.

Example C

```
      (woman) "Then I'm to take one of these after every meal and
               another at bedtime."
        (man) "That's right, and if the pain isn't gone by Monday,
               give me a call and we'll schedule another appointment."
(third voice) "Where did this conversation most probably take place?"
               A. In a department store
               B. In a law court
               C. In a doctor's office
               D. In a police station
```

Problems concerning locations provide a good change of pace, though the test writer must be sure to base such items on fairly universal experiences so as to avoid, or at least minimize, cultural bias.

Example D

```
        (man) "I understand that Paul has bought a farm and is trying
               to raise his own food.  How is it working out?"
      (woman) "The less said about that, the better!"
(third voice) "What did the woman probably mean by her answer?"
               A. That Paul didn't really buy a farm.
               B. That she hasn't heard much about Paul's farm.
               C. That Paul's farm hasn't been a success.
               D. That she is glad Paul bought the farm.
```

In the above item the speaker's mood and attitude are conveyed by a combination of colloquial language and "tone of voice." It is obviously a difficult item which would appear very close to the end of a comprehension test for advanced-level foreign learners of English.

5 *Testing Vocabulary*

SELECTION OF THE TEST WORDS

The selection of vocabulary test words is relatively easy in achievement tests, inasmuch as these can be drawn directly from the particular textbooks that have been used in class. In general proficiency testing, however, the problem of selecting appropriate lexical items is considerably more complicated, and it is with this problem that the following remarks will be concerned.

The first decision that must be made is whether to test the students' *active* or *passive* vocabulary—that is, the words they should be using in their speech and writing or those they will need merely to comprehend, especially in their reading. Generally speaking, vocabulary tests on an intermediate level will concentrate on the words needed in speaking or in comprehending the oral language, while tests on an advanced level will deal mostly with the lexicon of written English—the words needed by students if they are to understand newspapers, periodicals, literature, and textbooks.

Although the dictionary may be used in the selection of test words, it is generally more convenient to use word lists based on frequency counts of lexical items occurring in actual samples of the language. Two standard works dealing with the frequency of English words are Michael West's *A General Service List of English Words,*[1] a list with semantic frequencies of 2,000 words considered suitable as a basis of vocabulary for learning English as a second language, and Edward L. Thorndike and Irving Lorge's *The Teacher's Word Book of 30,000 Words,*[2] a much more extensive list which does not, however, indicate the relative frequency of the various *meanings* of the words it includes.

Useful as these and similar word counts are, the test maker must be alert to their several shortcomings:

1. Word counts are usually based on the written language only; therefore, many words that are extremely common in the oral language will receive low frequency ratings in the word lists. Thus, for example, in the *Teacher's Word Book* the words *bus* and *bathroom* are ranked in frequency with *treatise* and *compassion.*[3]

2. The word lists classify words according to relative frequency rather than absolute difficulty, and the two are by no means always equivalent. Thus, for example, the meaning of many derivatives (such as *examiner*, from *examine*) will be immediately evident to most examinees even though the derived forms may themselves be relatively infrequent in speech and writing.

3. Word frequency in English does not serve as a good guide to the probable difficulty of lexical items for which there are cognate forms in the foreign student's native language.

4. Some of the word lists do not differentiate among the various meanings of a word. Thus, although the item *bark* may be designated "very frequent," we cannot be sure that this designation would apply equally to the meanings "coverings of trees" and "the sound made by dogs," though we would be sure that it would definitely not apply to the meaning "a kind of sailing boat." The problem which this lack of data presents to the writer of vocabulary tests is obvious.

[1] London: Longmans, Green & Co., Ltd., 1953.

[2] New York: Teachers College Press, Columbia University, 1944.

[3] A new word count based on spoken English may prove of considerable value in the preparation of teaching and testing materials for foreign learners of English. It is Lyle V. Jones and Joseph M. Wepman's *A Spoken Word Count*, Chicago: Language Research Associates, 1966. For this count, 54 adult subjects were asked to tell a story about twenty pictures of the Thematic Apperception Test. From the corpus so collected, word frequency lists of several types were compiled, in one of which all distinct inflectional forms and grammatical uses were treated separately.

5. Unless the word lists are based on very recent surveys of frequency, they are likely to contain items whose status is currently quite different from what it was at the time the data were collected. Thus the *Teacher's Word Book*, based on a word count done between 1921 and 1931, classifies the words *television* and *atomic* as very infrequent.

6. Some word lists are based on a sample of written materials quite unlike those which the typical foreign learner of English is likely to have read. They may, for instance, have included large samples of unadapted "classics" whose language tends to be archaic. Thus the verb form *doth* is classified as more frequent than *airplane* in the *Teacher's Word Book*.

Despite these shortcomings, however, the standard word counts remain highly useful in the preparation of vocabulary tests so long as the test writer exercises reasonable judgment in interpreting the data. Frequency does, on the whole, constitute a fairly reliable index of difficulty and hence may serve as the basis upon which to compile lists of lexical items mostly likely to be appropriate for a given test population.

Before concluding this brief discussion of vocabulary selection, we must mention the problem of specialized vocabulary. Although there are many lexical items which most speakers of a language will use with about the same frequency, certain terms have far greater currency among the members of some professions and interest groups than among others. Unless a test is purposely devised for a specialized population (scientists, agricultural workers, teachers, or the like), the test writer should endeavor to restrict his vocabulary problems to terms in general use. A particularly common failing, in this connection, is the inclusion in general vocabulary tests of terms which discriminate against one sex or the other. Consider the following two lists of nouns, all given approximately the same frequency ratings in the *Teacher's Word Book*.

axle	blouse
filament	embroidery
fuse	gauze
gear	muslin
piston	quilt

transmission   shawl

valve   tassel

It may be assumed that the words in column 1 would generally be better understood by men than by women, while the words in column 2 pertain more commonly to feminine interests than to male. Test problems based on such specialized lexical items would tend to be biased and hence should be avoided in tests designed to measure general vocabulary control.

THE TESTING OF IDIOMS

Heretofore we have dealt exclusively with the testing of single words, but the test writer should consider the desirability of testing idioms as well. Of particular importance are the two-word verbs or verb-adverb combinations in which the English language abounds— idiomatic constructions such as *put off* (delay), *look over* (inspect), *come across* (encounter accidentally). The available word counts mentioned do not, unfortunately, provide information about the frequency of these combinations, and so the test writer will have to use his own judgment in selecting the forms to be tested.[4] All the item types described below lend themselves as well to the testing of such idioms as of single words.

ITEM TYPES

1. **Definition (multiple-choice).** What might be called the "classic" type of vocabulary item consists of a test word followed by several possible definitions or synonyms.[5]

nap

A. a brief sleep
B. a happy song
C. a sharp rock
D. a short meeting

[4]Fortunately, there are published collections of two-word verbs to which the test writer may refer, e.g., Thomas Lee Crowell, Jr., *A Glossary of Phrases with Prepositions*, 2d ed. Englewood Cliffs, N. J.: Prentice-Hall, Inc., 1960.

[5]In vocabulary tests for native speakers of English, antonym items have also been frequently used. However, the more direct synonym type appears to set a more relevant task in terms of everyday use of the language and is therefore generally regarded as preferable for the testing of foreign learners of English.

A variation of the foregoing reverses the order and places the definition first.

```
a brief, light sleep

A. nap
B. yawn
C. stroll
D. hug
```

Both versions of the definition item type have the advantage of being highly economical in terms both of the number of items that can be included on a printed page and of the number of problems that can be answered in a short period of testing time. Of the two versions, the second is generally preferable in that it permits the testing of several problem words per item. Moreover, version 2 items are more difficult to "compromise" by examinees who attempt systematically to memorize questions in order to reconstruct the test later.

On the negative side, tests consisting entirely of either version have one serious limitation: many words do not lend themselves to short, exact definitions or synonyms and cannot, therefore, be effectively tested by the above devices.

2. Completion (multiple-choice). A second item type places the problem words in context.

```
The old woman was too _____ to push open the heavy door.

A. feeble
B. sincere
C. deaf
D. harsh
```

Although requiring somewhat more space on the printed page and more time to answer, the above item type has the advantage of placing the problem words in a contextual setting, a procedure felt by many to provide a better measure of candidates' ability actually to use the test words actively in a real-life situation. Moreover, it allows the testing of many words which cannot be briefly defined as required in the previous type.[6]

---

[6] A variation of the above completion type identifies the alternatives only by their initials and an indication of the total number of letters. Thus for the previous example the choices might be presented as follows:

3. Paraphrase (multiple-choice). A third method of testing vocabulary, combining elements of two of the previously discussed devices, is to underline a word in context and provide several possible meanings.

```
John was astounded to hear her answer.

        A. greatly amused
        B. greatly relieved
        C. greatly surprised
        D. greatly angered
```

The advantage of this item type is, as with type 2, that it puts the test words in a context. Its chief disadvantages are that it allows the testing of only one problem word per item (though this need not be an overriding consideration) and is relatively easy to "compromise" by examinees who set out systematically to memorize the test words.

4. Paraphrase (supply type). A variation of type 3, requiring a structured short answer supplied by the examinee, is highly useful in informal classroom testing. In this type the problem sentence remains as above, but the examinees are asked to rewrite the sentence, substituting other words for the underlined portion. Thus, appropriate responses to the above problem would include "John was greatly surprised to hear her answer," "John was amazed to hear her answer," "John was astonished to hear her answer."

Vocabulary tests of this type are relatively easy to construct and, provided that students are instructed to give precise paraphrases, can quite effectively measure understanding of lexical items. Because examinees compose their own answers, this item type goes rather slowly, and students should not be expected to average more than one per minute. It is also a time-consuming type to score, inasmuch as the scorer will be required to make many judgments about the degree of appropriateness and the accuracy of the paraphrase. Because of such scoring problems, this item type is not recom-

```
        A. f-----
        B. s------
        C. d---
        D. h----
```

Proponents of this partial-clue type believe that, by concealing the choices in this manner, they are forcing the examinee to use his active, rather than passive, vocabulary. There are, however, at least two major criticisms of this item type. First, too much emphasis is placed on correct spelling, which should probably be tested separately, if at all. Secondly, candidates who check the "wrong" answer may have in mind a perfectly acceptable word that the test writer never thought of. (Thus in the above example, *scrawny, starved,* or *stunned* would fit choice B and be quite reasonable in the context.)

mended for most *mass testing* situations.

5. Pictures (objective). In the testing of children who have not yet reached the reading stage, vocabulary may be measured with pictures. Two types of picture items have frequently been used.

In the first type, the examiner pronounces the name of an object and asks the child to indicate, by pointing or making a pencil mark, which one of a set of pictures shows the object named. For example, the test booklet might contain four pictures—of a book, a bird, a boat, and a box—and the examiner might ask, "Draw a circle around the boat." In the second type, the child is shown a picture of an object and is asked to name it.

Either of these item types should function satisfactorily on the beginning level. The first, having a marked response, provides a permanent record of the child's performance and therefore does not require the examiner to stop and score the response himself. It is also conceivable that more than one child could be tested simultaneously in this way, though with small children individual testing may be preferable. A possible disadvantage of this item type is that the stimulus is oral, making such a test a measure of both vocabulary acquisition and listening comprehension, though probably on the elementary level this combination is logical and appropriate.

Picture tests need not, of course, be limited to nouns. Verbs, direction words, and other types of lexical items may also be tested (e.g., "Which boy is running?" "Where is the cat?"). These more expanded picture tests, however, should perhaps be regarded more as measures of listening comprehension and/or structural control than of "pure" vocabulary.

ADVICE ON ITEM WRITING

Inasmuch as it is not possible in this brief treatment to discuss the writing of all the types of vocabulary items mentioned above, we shall focus our attention on one typical item type, the simple definition plus test words (type 1, second version). All the principles discussed below can, however, be applied to one or more of the other item types as well.

1. The definition should be expressed in simple words readily comprehensible to all examinees.

Bad item   to inflict great anguish

                          A. precede
                          B. resent
                          C. adorn
                          D. torment

In the above example, the definition includes the words *inflict* and *anguish*, which may easily constitute comprehension problems as great as the test words in the choices. A general principle in vocabulary testing is to confine the comprehension problems to either the "lead" or the choices (depending on the item type selected), but not to insert problems in both. In the definition-plus-test-words item type, it is the alternatives that should provide the comprehension problems, not the definitions. We might revise the above definition to read: *to cause great suffering.*

2. All the alternatives should be on approximately the same level of difficulty.

Bad item   very evil

                          A. nefarious
                          B. delicious
                          C. prosperous
                          D. courageous

The correct answer, *nefarious*, would certainly be much more difficult for most examinees than the other choices.[7] Thus the correct answering of this item could mean only that the candidates were able to eliminate the three easier choices. A more equal set of choices would be:[8]

                          A. nefarious
                          B. precarious
                          C. delirious
                          D. gregarious

[7]Note that the derivative *courageous*, though listed as fairly infrequent in some of the word counts, is made easy by the frequency of the base form, *courage*.

[8]By making the item sounder, we have clearly increased its difficulty. As revised, the item would be appropriate only for very advanced learners of ESL. A much easier problem could be constructed around one of the original distracters:

                          very pleasing to the taste

                          A. prosperous
                          B. delicious
                          C. gracious
                          D. obvious

3. Whenever possible, all choices should be related to the same general area or kind of activity.

Bad item   a small branch

> A. twig
> B. frog
> C. doom
> D. plum

An examinee who knows only that he has seen *twig* in writings about the woods could answer the above item correctly. The following set of choices would probably strengthen the item, inasmuch as they are all related to trees and other growing things:

> A. twig
> B. shrub
> C. reed
> D. wreath

4. The choices in each item should be of approximately the same length or be paired by length. No single choice should attract attention merely because it looks unlike the others in the set.

Bad item   to think deeply about

> A. vex
> B. poll
> C. tug
> D. contemplate

In the above item, choice D is so different in appearance from the others that the problem-solving task has been complicated by the insertion of a purely visual factor. It cannot be predicted exactly how examinees will react to the different-looking alternative: some will suspect that it must be the right answer, and others will want to avoid it. It is better item-writing practice to avoid such extraneous factors by using a set of choices more balanced in appearance.

All one-syllable words	*Alternately one- and two-syllable words*
A. grab	A. bliss
B. punch	B. concord
C. dodge	C. poise
D. shove	D. pretense

5. Items should be kept free of extraneous spelling problems. That is, no attempt should be made to mislead examinees with distracters that look or sound like possible right answers.

Bad item   to cook by exposing to direct heat

                A. roost
                B. strew
                C. fray
                D. broil

The above item, though deliberately exaggerated for purposes of emphasis, illustrates a common tendency of some less experienced item writers. Excessive trickiness is simply not necessary in language testing, and, what is more important, it will generally becloud the issue by combining two or more kinds of problems in a single item—in this case, lexical meaning and spelling.

6

Testing Reading Comprehension

WHAT IS MEANT BY READING COMPREHENSION

When we come to the testing of reading comprehension, we are concerned with the testing of students who have passed beyond the purely audio-lingual state of language learning, in which "reading" and "writing" are used simply to reinforce the oral/aural learnings, and have proceeded to a stage in which reading and writing are taught as skills (or, more properly, as complexes of skills) recognized as useful in themselves. Because of the importance of this point, let us amplify it a bit.

In most modern foreign language courses, instruction begins with the teaching of the sound system and the most frequent and/or useful grammatical patterns of the spoken language. Vocabulary is at first quite limited, but as the student gains control over the sounds and structures of the language, he is "fed" more and more vocabulary, chosen for its usefulness in oral communication. During this stage, such reading as is presented to the student is designed primarily to strengthen his control of the oral/aural skills. Readings are generally built around the grammatical structures and lexical items which the student will need to communicate orally, and the content of the material is regarded as relatively unimportant. When the teacher considers that his class has gained a good functional control of the spoken language, he may introduce reading as an end in itself. At this point the class enters an area where some students will undoubtedly advance much faster and much further than others, for reading involves, for both native speaker and foreign learner, the manipulation of a complex of skills only part of which are, strictly speaking, linguistic. The abilities needed in reading a language include at least the following:

1. **Language and graphic symbols**
   a. Comprehending a large percentage of the lexical items occurring in nonspecialized writing and being able to derive the meaning of unfamiliar items (or special uses of common items) from the contexts in which they occur
   b. Understanding the syntactical patterns and morphological forms characteristic of the written language and following the longer and more involved stretches of language (sentences and sequences of sentences) occurring in formal writing
   c. Responding correctly to the graphic symbols of writing (e.g., punctuation, capitalization, paragraphing, italicizing) used to convey and clarify meaning
2. **Ideas**
   a. Identifying the writer's purpose and central idea
   b. Understanding the subordinate ideas which support the thesis
   c. Drawing correct conclusions and valid inferences from what is given
3. **Tone and style**
   a. Recognizing the author's attitude toward the subject and the reader; understanding the tone of the writing
   b. Identifying the methods and stylistic devices by which the author conveys his ideas

In practice, the above abilities are mutually dependent. A writer may, for example, elect to use humor (3a) to make the reader aware of some common human failing (2a), conveying the ludicrousness of this human behavior by an unusual selection of lexical items (1a). The good reader, then, is one who can respond simultaneously—and appropriately—to the language, ideas, and stylistics of mature writing, and, moreover, can achieve these understandings *with reasonable speed and fluency.*[1] It is the foreign student's acquisition of such a complex of abilities that we wish to measure in reading comprehension tests.

GENERAL FORM OF THE READING TEST

It has been found that the same general type of test long used to measure the reading ability of native speakers of English will work with equal effectiveness with foreign learners of the language. Such a test consists of a number of short passages of varying styles and content, each followed by a series of multiple-choice comprehension items.[2] By a judicious selection of his passages and a careful working of his items, the test writer is able to test the examinee's understanding not only of the surface meaning of a passage but also of the author's purpose, attitude, and method—in fact, all the abilities listed in the previous section. Thus the reading comprehension test is somewhat parallel to the advanced-level auditory comprehension test in which the student is given rather long stretches of the oral language, perhaps in the form of dialogues, from which he must sift out and interpret a multiplicity of phonological, grammatical, and lexical signals occurring simultaneously.

SELECTION OF THE TEST PASSAGES

1. **Length.** Inasmuch as the test writer will generally wish to include samples of various kinds of material, the individual test passages should be kept brief. On the other hand, there should be sufficient content to yield at least six or seven comprehension items for pretesting. Passages of between 100 and 250 words are about the proper length.

2. **Subject matter.** The specific purpose of the test will naturally dictate the subject matter of the passages selected. In a general screening test for foreign applicants to American universities, for instance, the selections should reflect the various kinds of reading material assigned in basic university courses. For these the test writer may draw upon such works as biographies, prose fiction,

---

[1]The matter of reading rate will be considered in a later section of this chapter.
[2]These items may consist either of questions followed by several possible answers or of incomplete statements with several possible completions.

encyclopedia entries, and nontechnical articles on the natural and social sciences.

The excerpts must be clear and meaningful when taken out of context, and not require outside subject-matter information to be fully comprehended. It cannot usually be assumed, for example, that the examinees will have the same kind of knowledge of American history, traditions, and cultural patterns as the American-born student. Nor should the subject matter be such as to give a marked advantage to students in particular fields (unless, of course, the test is designed for a special group of students such as science or education majors). On the other hand, the passages should not deal with information that is universally known, for in this case the candidates may be able to answer the questions correctly without paying much attention to the passages. (Thus a paragraph dealing in a general way with a widely known historical event or personage would constitute an unreliable test of reading comprehension.)

3. **Style and treatment of subject.** As already suggested, reading tests should generally include materials of various types and styles, though all should possess reasonable merit as pieces of writing. The test writer will soon learn, however, that the literary excellence of a paragraph is not in itself a guarantee of its suitability as a test passage. Paragraphs that make just one clear, direct point, for instance, seldom make suitable passages for testing purposes, inasmuch as they do not yield a sufficient number of test items. Much more likely are paragraphs which (*a*) deal chronologically with a series of events, (*b*) compare or contrast two or more people, objects, or events, *(c)* present an author's individualistic opinions on a familiar subject.

4. **Language.** Although, as stated above, the passages in a reading test should approximate materials which the examinees are likely to encounter when they put their English to use, the test writer must always set realistic tasks for his test population, which consists, after all, of learners of a second, or foreign, language. Therefore, passages that are overloaded with extremely difficult lexical items and/or complex syntactical structures may have to be adapted somewhat to bring them within reach of at least the more proficient candidates. The simplification of reading passages must, however, be carefully

controlled lest the test be made so easy that it fails to discriminate between students on various levels of proficiency.[3]

ADVICE ON ITEM WRITING

1. The vocabulary and syntax of the items should be kept as simple as possible so that the real problem is the interpretation of the *passage*, not of the questions that are asked about it.

2. Insofar as possible, the "stem" or "lead" of the item should establish the problem—that is, make clear what kind of information is being asked for.

Bad item   John

    A. obviously liked what he heard
    B. became angry upon hearing Mary's words
    C. didn't understand what he was told
    D. ridiculed Mary's ideas

In the above example, the stem is merely the word *John*, which offers no clues to the reader as to what he is being asked. The above item might be rewritten:

It was clear from John's reactions to Mary's speech that he

    A. agreed completely with what she had said
    B. found her remarks highly insulting
    C. really didn't understand what she had said
    D. considered her ideas to be quite foolish

3. Selection of the correct answer should involve *interpretation* of the passage, not merely matching the words in the choices with the same words in the paragraph.

Passage and bad item

Early the next morning I received yet another letter from Roger, informing me that he was still confined to his bed with the same mysterious illness and urging me to come to his aid. I set forth at once for Portsmouth, arriving shortly before dusk. I went

---

[3] A good advanced-level reading test for foreign students will generally include some items that even many native speakers of English would miss, for, as we have already noted, reading is not one of the language skills that everyone learns to master, even in the first language. On the other hand, if the entire test proved difficult for mature native speakers of English, we would scarcely be justified in calling it a test of English as a second language.

with all possible haste to High Street and thence to the familiar old house, which appeared in no way altered since the days of my previous visit. Yet upon entering, I was amazed to find its dark, cavernous rooms completely deserted!

```
When the writer found Roger's house deserted, he felt
    A. angry
    B. relieved
    C. amazed
    D. happy
```

This item involves a mere matching of words: *amazed* is the term used in both the passage and the test item. A less superficial testing of comprehension would be:

> The writer mentions his surprise at
>   A. receiving a letter from Roger
>   B. learning of Roger's illness
>   C. seeing the appearance of Roger's house
>   D. finding that Roger was not at home

4. All items should require a careful reading of the paragraph. It should not be possible to answer items correctly purely on the basis of outside knowledge or to eliminate some of the choices because they are clearly illogical or because they conflict with one another.

Bad item
>   We may infer from this paragraph that people
>   A. all need the same kind of rest
>   B. do not usually need rest
>   C. rest much more than they should
>   D. do not all rest in the same way

Choice B is patently absurd and can therefore be dismissed without reference to the passage. Choices A and D are clearly opposites, leading the test-wise examinee to suspect that one of them is the correct answer. On the basis of logic, D would appear to be the more likely answer. Choice D would also seem more likely to be true than choice C.

The above item, which appeared in a reading test for foreign students, shows how poor items can often be answered by pure reason without reading the passages on which they are based. This item might be rewritten:

The central idea of the paragraph is that people

A. cannot maintain good health without proper rest
B. do not all rest in precisely the same way
C. tend to get more rest than they actually need
D. can rest better after they have had exercise

As revised, all four choices appear logical. The examinee must therefore understand the paragraph to know which of them constituted the central idea.

ASSEMBLING THE FINAL FORM

After the reading items have been pretested, some will probably have to be eliminated on the basis of the item analysis (see Chapter 9). If too few items remain for a given passage, it will be necessary to discard the entire set. There is no established rule on how many comprehension items should accompany a passage, but there should be a reasonable relation between the length of the passage and the number of questions asked about it. Thus, for example, it would clearly be inefficient to include a 250-word passage with only two items. On the other hand, a 100-word passage with four items would usually be regarded as quite satisfactory. If, as recommended above, passages range generally from 100 to 250 words, we would hope that each passage would be followed by four to seven items, and more if possible. With this sort of distribution, we would probably be safe in allowing one minute of testing time per item, including in this figure the time needed by the examinee to read and reread the passages. Such a test would allow sufficient time for the average reader but would provide a justifiable penalty for those most seriously handicapped by their inefficient reading speeds.[4] From the figure of

---

[4] The *Test of English as a Foreign Language* (*TOEFL*) is somewhat more generous in allowing forty minutes for the working of 30 comprehension problems, although time for

one item per minute it will be observed that reading comprehension measures go slower than almost any other kind of language test, and therefore they generally contain relatively few items. To be reliable even as a subtest within a much longer examination, our reading test should include at least 30 items, or about five passages.[5] And if the reading test is to be used by itself as the basis for decision making about individual students, it should certainly contain more than our minimum of 30 items. One solution is to combine vocabulary and reading to form one long test or subtest, and this logical combination is often used in the standard language tests.

SAMPLE READING PASSAGE AND ITEMS

The following passage and set of comprehension items will serve to illustrate the principles that were discussed above.

In the development of literature, prose generally comes late. Verse is more effective for oral delivery and more easily retained in the memory. It is therefore a rather remarkable fact that English possessed a considerable body of prose literature in the ninth century, at a time when most other modern languages in Europe had barely developed a literature in verse. This unusual accomplishment was due to the inspiration of one man, King Alfred the Great, who ruled from 871 to 899. When he came to the throne, Alfred found that the learning which in the previous century had placed England in the forefront of Europe had greatly decayed. In an effort to restore his country to something like its former state, he undertook to provide for his people certain books in English, books which he deemed most essential to

---

reading the directions is included in the forty minutes. On the average, about 92 percent of *TOEFL* candidates complete the reading comprehension subtest within the time limits. *(Test of English as a Foreign Language: Interpretive Information,* New York: College Entrance Examination Board, Princeton, N.J.: Educational Testing Service, 1967, p. 15.)
[5] Based on the experience of *TOEFL*, we could anticipate that a well-written, 30-item reading subtest would have a reliability coefficient of about .85. For so short a test, this is very satisfactory reliability. (High reliability depends in part, of course, on the soundness of the individual items.)

their welfare. In preparation for this task, he set about in mature life to learn Latin.[6]

1. According to the information given in the paragraph, King Alfred may most properly be regarded as the father of English
    A. poetry
    B. learning
    C. prose
    D. literature
2. The writer suggests that the earliest English poetry was
    A. written in very difficult language
    B. not intended to be read silently
    C. never really popular with the public
    D. less original than later poetry
3. According to the paragraph, England's learning had brought it to the "forefront of Europe" (line 10) in the
    A. seventh century
    B. eighth century
    C. ninth century
    D. tenth century
4. The writer suggests that at the time of King Alfred most of the other modern languages of Europe had
    A. both a verse and a prose literature
    B. a literature in prose but not in verse
    C. neither a prose nor a verse literature
    D. a literature in verse but not in prose
5. We may conclude from the paragraph that the books which Alfred "deemed most essential" were
    A. already available in another language
    B. written largely in verse
    C. later translated into Latin
    D. original with Alfred himself

---

[6] Adapted from *A History of the English Language*, 2d ed., by Albert C. Baugh. Copyright© 1957 by Appleton-Century-Crofts, Inc. Reprinted by permission of Appleton-Century-Crofts, Inc., and the author.

The above set consists of a short paragraph (about 155 words) followed by five comprehension items—a good balance between length of passage and number of items. Though the passage is admittedly a fairly difficult one—such as might appear at the end of a reading test for advanced-level foreign students of English—most of the lexical items fall within the first 4,000 words of the Thorndike-Lorge word count[7] or are derivatives of more frequent forms, such as *accomplishment* and *inspiration*. Four less frequent items which might cause comprehension difficulties are *prose, oral, forefront,* and *mature*. To these may be added the idiom "set about" and a few common words that are here used in a special sense: (oral) *delivery, body* (of literature), and *state* (of being). Context, however, surely provides a clue to the meaning of most of these.

In contrast to the passage, the five comprehension problems employ only fairly frequent vocabulary items. The problems are designed to cover the main points of the paragraph:

1. That in modern European cultures, including that of England, verse preceded prose because the former lent itself better to oral transmission
2. That English learning had reached a high state in the eighth century and then declined in the ninth
3. That Alfred set about developing English prose in order to revive learning
4. That much of the early English prose was borrowed from Latin, some by Alfred himself
5. That, through Alfred's efforts, England acquired a prose literature before most of the other modern European states

The five multiple-choice items testing these points are all of the incomplete-sentence type, the stem or lead generally setting up the specific problem in some detail.

[7] See p. 49 above.

Testing Writing

WHAT IS MEANT BY "WRITING"

As pointed out at the beginning of the previous chapter, the teaching of writing as an integrated process will, like the teaching of reading, normally be deferred until rather advanced courses in English as a second language. During the early stages of learning, written exercises will generally be used simply to reinforce the learning of specific grammatical points or lexical items; only later will writing be treated as an end in itself—as a complex skill involving the simultaneous practice of a number of very different abilities, some of which are never fully achieved by many students, even in their native language.

Although the writing process has been analyzed in many different ways, most teachers would probably agree in recognizing at least the following five general components:

1. **Content**: the substance of the writing; the ideas expressed
2. **Form**: the organization of the content

3. **Grammar**: the employment of grammatical forms and syntactic patterns
4. **Style**: the choice of structures and lexical items to give a particular tone or flavor to the writing
5. **Mechanics**: the use of the graphic conventions of the language

From the above we see that the writing process, as commonly conceived, is a highly sophisticated skill combining a number of diverse elements, only some of which are strictly linguistic.

COMPARISON OF COMPOSITION AND OBJECTIVE TESTS OF WRITING

It would seem obvious that the most direct way of measuring students' writing ability would be to have them write. Yet, as all language teachers are surely aware, there has in the past fifty years been much criticism of the conventional essay test on the part of educational-measurement specialists. And this criticism has, in turn, brought forth a very spirited defense of the essay examination by many teachers and educationists.

Those who have championed the essay or composition have generally included the following points in their defense:[1]

1. Composition tests require students to organize their own answers, expressed in their own words. Thus composition tests measure certain writing abilities (e.g., ability to organize, relate, and weigh materials) more effectively than do objective tests.

2. Composition tests motivate students to improve their writing; conversely, if examinations do not require writing, many students will neglect the development of this skill.

3. Composition tests are much easier and quicker to prepare than objective tests, an important advantage to the busy classroom teacher.

The critics of composition testing have usually answered along the following lines:

1. Composition tests are unreliable measures because (1) students perform differently on different topics and on different occasions; and (2) the scoring of compositions is by nature highly subjective.

[1] We shall consider only those arguments that are directly relevant to *language* testing.

2. In writing compositions, students can cover up weaknesses by avoiding problems (e.g., the use of certain grammatical patterns and lexical items) they find difficult. Such evasion is impossible with well-prepared objective tests.

3. Composition tests require much more scoring time than objective tests; for this reason, compositions add greatly to the expense and administrative problems of large-scale testing.

It is unfortunate that, in this long-standing debate, many people have adopted fixed attitudes on one side or the other and have failed to keep abreast of, or have ignored, a number of new studies which definitely provide a basis for reconciliation. The current "moderate position" in regard to testing writing ability, based on recent findings, may be summarized as follows:

1. Well-constructed objective tests of the language skills have been found to correlate quite highly with general writing ability, as determined by the rating of actual samples of free writing.[2] Thus in situations where the scoring of compositions would be unfeasible (as in some large-scale testing operations), objective tests can be used alone as fairly good predictors of general writing skill.

2. At the same time, it is now clear that there are ways to administer and score composition tests so that they, too, may be used by themselves as reliable instruments. Put briefly, high reliability can be obtained by taking several samples of writing from each student and having each sample read by several trained readers.[3] Thus the classroom teacher who lacks the experience and/or the time

[2]For example, a 1961 study undertaken for the College Entrance Examination Board showed that sixty-minute objective tests specifically designed to measure writing skills can be made to correlate above .70 with a reliable criterion of composition scores. (Fred I. Godshalk, Frances Swineford, and William E. Coffman, *Studies of the Question Types in the CEEB English Composition Test as Predictors of an Essay Criterion*, Statistical Analysis Report 65-20, Princeton, N.J.: Educational Testing Service, 1965, p. 22.) A study carried out for the *Test of English as a Foreign Language* (*TOEFL*) in 1966 showed similar results: the forty-minute writing ability subtest of *TOEFL* was found to correlate .74 with a criterion of four short compositions, each of which was rated by two English teachers. (*Test of English as a Foreign Language: Interpretive Information*, New York: College Entrance Examination Board; Princeton, N.J.: Educational Testing Service, 1967, p. 18.)

[3]For example, in the 1961 College Board study it was found that when five twenty-minute essays were scored independently by five raters, the approximate scorer reliability was .92 and the test reliability was about .84. In contrast, when just one twenty-minute essay was read by only one reader, the scorer and test reliability indices were only about .40 and .25 respectively. (Godshalk, Swineford, and Coffman, *op. cit.*, p. 48. See also *Test of English as a Foreign Language: Interpretive Information, ibid.)* Although testing specialists have for some time advocated multiple scoring of several compositions per candidate, only recently has the soundness of this procedure been tested, and confirmed, by rigorous, comprehensive experiments.

to construct objective tests of writing ability, or who feels strongly about the pedagogical value of testing writing through writing, can use compositions with a reasonable degree of confidence.

3. Inasmuch as both objective tests and composition tests have their own special strengths, the ideal practice is undoubtedly to measure writing skill with a combination of the two types of tests, and it is recommended that this procedure be followed whenever conditions permit. Such a combination will probably produce somewhat more valid results than would either of the two types of measures used by itself.

In accordance with the foregoing, we shall devote the remainder of this chapter first to examining types of objective tests that might be used to measure writing ability and then to describing methods of improving the composition test.

OBJECTIVE TESTS OF THE ELEMENTS OF WRITING

Testing Formal Grammar and Style

As we noted in Chapter 3, the kinds of grammatical problems that are tested in objective *writing-ability tests* differ markedly from the problems included in *structure tests* for foreign students. In the latter tests we are concerned with measuring control of the basic grammatical patterns of the language. In our structure items, therefore, the contrast is between English and non-English, and we would assume that a native speaker would, except through careless-ness, score 100 percent correct. In our measures of writing ability, on the other hand, we are testing sensitivity to the grammatical patterns appropriate to the written, as contrasted with the spoken, form of the language, and we would suppose that many native speakers would fail to make some of the distinctions. Examples of the kinds of formal grammatical matters that we might include in our tests of writing ability—but not in structure tests—are the following:

Subject-verb agreement

The design of the two new bridges (are/is) very unusual.

Structural parallelism

She enjoyed sewing, reading, and just (to sit/sitting) on the porch watching the people go by.

Case of pronouns

To my little brother and (I/me), Uncle John was the most wonderful friend.

Comparison of adjectives

The afternoon rush hour is the (worse/worst) part of the day in which to drive through the city.

Formation of adverbs

The man tipped his hat and spoke very (polite/politely) to the ladies.

Formation of irregular verbs

Neither of the children would tell us who had (broke/broken) the window.

If some of these problems seem too reminiscent of "traditional" or "prescriptive" grammar, it must be understood that our goal is to determine how acceptable the foreign student's written English will be to the native speakers of English who will read his compositions, letters of application, business communications, and the like. Whether for good or ill, most of these readers will be applying very conservative criteria. Therefore, if our advanced-level test is to have relevance and validity, it should undoubtedly contain the kinds of formal grammatical points by which the student will subsequently be judged in real-life situations. What is vitally important is that such a test be clearly identified, by its title, directions, and problem contexts, as a measure of *writing skill* and not be confused with tests of basic structural control.[4]

In addition to control of grammatical forms and syntactic

---

[4]It is a common fault of writing-ability tests that formal grammatical points are tested within highly colloquial contexts. The following examples of such confusion of levels of usage are from published tests for native speakers of English:

Do not yell (like) (as if) you were having a tooth pulled.

If anybody calls, tell (them) (him) I'll return at four o'clock.

In such items the better students could very logically select the "wrong answer," except that they generally know how the test writer wishes them to respond.

patterns, effective written expression depends on the writer's lexical resources. The vocabulary tests described in Chapter 5 will certainly have some relevance in measuring the foreign student's writing ability. Such tests, however, are usually concerned only with general meanings, and good writing requires considerable precision in the use of lexical items. Specifically, the writer must be fully aware of the "social status" and connotative meanings of the items he uses and must be able to combine them felicitously into phrases and longer units. Thus, for instance, although it is true that the words *companion, comrade, chum,* and *crony* all carry the same general "meaning" and may all be listed as synonyms in the student's pocket bilingual dictionary, he will certainly run into trouble if he attempts to use them interchangeably. Comprehensive tests of writing skill therefore require attention to appropriate style and diction as illustrated by the following examples.

The two new senators have proved themselves exceptionally able (guys/men).

We were unable to determine what the real significance of his remarks (meant/was).

Poor Mr. Baker has been ill (the bulk of/the greater part of) his life.

During the speeches, the need for reform in government was (laid stress on/emphasized).

Because of his obvious sincerity and the direct appeal of his arguments, the mayor's proposals have (secured a good foothold in the eyes of the people/won the strong support of the people).

Having taken note of some of the factors to be considered in choosing problems of grammar and style for our tests of writing ability, let us now consider a few specific item types.

1. **Error recognition.** The examinee is required to indicate which of several underlined parts of a sentence is unacceptable for formal written English, or to indicate that the sentence contains no "error."

The position taken in his most recent speeches seem to indicate a will-
            A   B   C
ingness to compromise. No error.
       D   E

This item type puts the examinee in the position of a reader who must make judgments about the acceptability of a piece of writing and identify any point of weakness. As such it has sometimes been objected to on the grounds that the examinee (1) does not have to prove ability to correct the errors he finds, and (2) may possibly choose the correct answer for the wrong reason. Despite these theoretical objections, however, experience would seem to indicate that error-recognition items function as well as those which require the examinee to select from among several alternative methods of expression.[5] To ensure comprehensive coverage, the test writer would probably do well to combine an error-recognition subtest with a sentence-completion or sentence-correction subtest in his measure of writing ability.

2. **Sentence completion.** The examinee is required to select the best way of completing a sentence in terms of grammar, diction, tone, and sense.

```
During his last year in office, his popularity with the voters _____.

    A. descended downward swiftly
    B. quickly touched bottom
    C. declined very suddenly
    D. rapidly plunged under
```

This item type provides an excellent method of measuring a wide range of problems relating to the effective use of written English. It is probably the most commonly used of the multiple-choice techniques for testing sensitivity to appropriate style in writing.

3. **Sentence correction.** The examinee is required to select the best revision of an underlined portion of a sentence. If the sentence is acceptable as it stands, the examinee selects choice A, which is always identical to the underlined portion of the sentence.

```
While watching from our window, the great ship slowly entered the harbor,
whistle blowing and crew cheering.

    A. While watching
    B. Upon watching
    C. As we watched
    D. Having been watched
```

This item type combines features of types 1 and 2. The examinee is asked first to judge the acceptability of one feature (usually a structural point) of an existing sentence and then, if he finds that

---

[5] The recent College Board study of the correlations between objective tests and scored compositions showed the same results for the error-recognition and sentence-correction tests: both correlated .71 with the essay criterion. (Godshalk, Swineford, and Coffman, *op. cit.*, p. 21.)

feature inappropriate, to choose the best of several corrections. As
such, this technique provides an interesting variation of the two
foregoing types, though in practice it seems to lack the flexibility of
type 2, which is used to test sensitivity to style as well as structure.

Testing the Ability to Organize Materials

It cannot be claimed that wholly successful objective techniques
have yet been found for testing the student's ability to organize his
ideas into unified, coherent written presentations, and perhaps this
goal will always lie beyond the tester's reach.[6] Probably the most
satisfactory of the tests that we do have are those of paragraph
organization, in which the examinee is required to reorder several
"scrambled" sentences into a coherent paragraph, and to indicate the
correct order of the sentences.

A. The report from Stratford that he "spent at the rate of a thousand pounds
   a year" is surely very far from the truth, being based no doubt on Stratford gossip.

B. On this income we may be sure that he lived well and comfortably in Stratford.

C. It is difficult to estimate Shakespeare's income in his last years.

D. Probably Shakespeare received from all sources less than a quarter of
   that sum, say two hundred pounds.

Which sentence did you put <u>first</u>?   A   B Ⓒ D
Which sentence did you put <u>second</u>? Ⓐ B   C   D
Which sentence did you put <u>third</u>?   A   B   C Ⓓ
Which sentence did you put <u>last</u>?   A Ⓑ C   D

Although the paragraph organization items undoubtedly are
useful in testing the student's understanding of certain ordering
devices of English, such as the sequence signals,[7] they must be
considered relatively narrow, if not superficial, measures of organ-
izing ability. Moreover, it is extremely difficult to find or compose
paragraphs which can be reordered in just one acceptable way. As a
consequence, paragraph organization items have been found less
effective as predictors of general writing skill than the item types

---

[6]Indeed, it is still not clear whether there really *is* such a thing as "general ability to
organize," nor has it been conclusively demonstrated that "judges can agree very closely on
the quality of organization shown in a particular set of students' papers prepared under test
conditions." (John M. Stalnaker, "The Essay Type of Examination," in E. F. Lindquist
(ed.), *Educational Measurement*, Washington: American Council on Education, 1951, p.
509.)

[7]Sequence signals occurring in our sample paragraph organization items are the words *he* in
sentences A and B, *this* in sentence B, and *that* in sentence D.

described in the preceding section.[8] This fact need not necessarily rule out the use of objective tests of organization, but it does strongly suggest that they should always be used in conjunction with other measures, such as those discussed previously.

Testing the Mechanics of Writing

Punctuation and capitalization, the so-called mechanics of writing, may be tested objectively with simple adaptations of the completion and correction items described earlier. The following example illustrates one common technique.

```
Directions--Decide what punctuation, if any, should be used in the num-
bered spaces, and indicate the letter that goes with your choice. ("N"
means "no punctuation.")

Returning to his friend Peter Bill asked whether he still wished to con-
tinue with the trip              1             2
                    3
```

1-A ;	2-A ;	3-A ?
1-B :	2-B ,"	3-B ?"
1-C ,	2-C ;"	3-C .
1-D .	2-D N	3-D ."

In preparing tests of the mechanics of writing, one must be careful to avoid testing matters of divided usage. Particularly in the case of punctuation, there are really only a very limited number of points on which there is universal agreement. Substantial differences will be found among the leading publishers within the United States, and the differences between American and British practice can be even more dramatic. The last point is particularly important in the testing of foreign students, who may have learned to follow British models in their writing. Note, for example, the following two versions of the same sentence, the first punctuated in the more usual American fashion, and the second as it might appear in a British publication:

"I'll return at 4:30," Dr. Smith replied.
'I'll return at 4.30', Dr Smith replied.

Clearly, then, if the test writer wishes to include problems of mechanics in his test of writing ability, he must be aware of the admissible variations in practice and frame his items so that only one

---

[8]See Godshalk, Swineford, and Coffman, *loc. cit.*

alternative could be an acceptable answer.

Closely related to the so-called mechanics, though allowing of far less variation, is spelling. Although objective spelling items have the advantage of being easy to prepare, there are several reasons for questioning their appropriateness in a general test of writing ability. First, it is unlikely that good writers are necessarily good spellers. Secondly, in almost any practical writing situation the student will be able to consult a dictionary. And thirdly, the common testing method of asking the examinee to identify the one misspelled word in each group of four or five lexical items may be an unreliable kind of measurement: most of us have had the experience of looking so hard at printed words that we lose the ability to judge their correctness. All in all, one would certainly be justified in omitting spelling problems from objective tests of writing skill.

IMPROVING THE EFFECTIVENESS OF COMPOSITION TESTS

So much attention has been given to the problems of improving composition measures within the past few decades that a thorough treatment of the subject would almost require a book in itself. We shall here attempt to do no more than summarize briefly those conclusions which appear of greatest value to the classroom teacher who wishes to improve the design and scoring of his own tests.[9]

Preparation of the Test

1. **Arrange to take several samples, rather than just one.** Normally two or more short compositions will prove to be more reliable than one long one. And having the compositions written at different times will yield better results than having them written at one sitting.

2. **Set writing tasks that are within the reach of all.** Although we should of course endeavor to select composition topics of interest and challenge to the better students, we must avoid setting tasks that require a high degree of ingenuity and creativity. The purpose of general writing-ability testing is to elicit characteristic samples of every student's writing and from these to determine his proficiency

[9]For additional treatments, the reader is referred to Stalnaker, *op. cit.*, chap. 13; and Robert L. Thorndike and Elizabeth Hagen, *Measurement and Evaluation in Psychology and Education*, 2d ed. New York: John Wiley & Sons, Inc., 1961, pp. 27-57.

at expressing himself in clear, effective, and grammatical prose—not to measure his "creative powers."[10]   Topics which call for straightforward narrative or description are most likely to accomplish the above objectives.

3. Make the writing tasks clear and specific; provide full directions. A vague writing assignment such as "Write a theme about friendship" not only will lead to nonequivalent performances but will cause many students to waste valuable time just getting started. Thus it is highly important to write the composition question in such a way that the task is clearly and unambiguously defined for each examinee.

Example:

> Describe an interesting member of your family: one of your parents or grandparents, a brother or sister, cousin, aunt, or uncle. Be specific in describing the special characteristics that you think make him or her an interesting person. You may wish to give examples of things this person has said or done which illustrate these characteristics.

4. Allow no alternatives. If some students are performing different tasks from others, it is difficult to compare performances or to ensure that all students have undertaken equivalent tasks.

5. Pretest the writing test assignments, if only on yourself, to be sure that they are really workable and are realistic in terms of the time available to the students. It is very useful, in this connection, to keep a file of topics which have been used and found to be particularly effective. Once a sizable pool of successful topics has been built up, they may be drawn upon in the preparation of important tests.

Scoring the Test

1. Decide in advance on the precise basis for scoring. The starting point is to decide on the weight or emphasis that will be given to each of the various writing factors, such as content, form, grammar, style, and mechanics. The actual rating of the compositions may then consist either of (*a*) allotting a specified number of points to each of the factors, the total of the factor ratings constituting the

---

[10] Moreover, whatever "creative ability" really is—and there is no consensus on a precise definition—it is most probably too unstable a characteristic always to be on call in a testing situation.

composition score,[11] or (b) making a general, overall judgment of each composition and placing it in one of four or more categories (e.g., 1, poor; 2, fair; 3, good; 4, excellent) based not on any notion of an absolute standard, but in terms of the performance of the group as a whole.

In the usual classroom situation, where only one teacher is scoring a set of his own compositions, the first system is perhaps the more useful. Where several readers are available to rate each composition, the "general impression" method of scoring can actually yield more reliable results.

2. If possible, treat the papers anonymously during scoring. In very small classes, of course, anonymous scoring is extremely difficult if not impossible, for the teacher will recognize his students by their handwriting and style. When numbers permit, however, anonymous scoring is highly desirable, for identification of papers often leads quite unconsciously to scorer bias. Papers may be scored anonymously simply by having the students put their names on the unused backs of the sheets or on the cover of the test booklets, which may all be folded back before scoring begins.

3. Before marking any papers, scan a sample of papers to decide upon standards. Find, for example, a high, high-medium, low-medium, and low paper to serve as models. Then, as you score the papers, return occasionally to your models to ensure that your standards are not shifting.

4. If the compositions are to be used to make critical decisions about large numbers of students (as, for instance, in a common departmental final examination) (a) have at least two independent readers for each theme; (b) begin with a practice session for all readers in which they agree together on the rating of a sample of papers so as to establish common standards; (c) make the grade for each composition the *sum* or the *average* of the ratings of the two or more readers. It is sometimes the practice, when the ratings of two readers do not agree, to have the paper read a third time, and then to

---

[11] For this purpose some teachers have devised scoring grids which are attached to the compositions. These list the factors that will be considered in scoring, each rated on a 0-5 or 0-6 point basis. While recent experiments may raise some question as to whether this system is as effective in large-scale testing as the "general impression" method, the scoring grid is probably a good classroom device in that it helps the teacher to maintain a consistent scoring procedure, enables the students to know in advance what the basis of the scoring will be, and—on the teaching side—directs students' attention to specific areas of strength and weakness.

accept whichever rating is nearer to that of the third reader. Experiments have shown, however, that this practice makes the grade less reliable than when the simple sum or average of the two ratings is taken.

8 *Testing Oral Production*

WHAT IS MEANT BY SPEAKING A SECOND LANGUAGE

No language skill is so difficult to assess with precision as speaking ability, and for this reason it seemed wise to defer our consideration of oral production tests until last. Moreover, some of the problems involved in the evaluation of speaking skill occur (though generally with less severity) in other forms of language testing, and hence the preceding chapters may serve to orient the reader somewhat.

Like writing, speaking is a complex skill requiring the simultaneous use of a number of different abilities which often develop at different rates. Either four or five components are generally recognized in analyses of the speech process:

1. **Pronunciation** (including the segmental features—vowels and consonants—and the stress and intonation patterns)
2. **Grammar**
3. **Vocabulary**
4. **Fluency** (the ease and speed of the flow of speech)

To these should probably be added (5) **Comprehension**, for oral communication certainly requires a subject to respond to speech as well as to initiate it.

If we compare the above inventory with that which was presented in the preceding chapter on the testing of writing, one essential difference is apparent. As used in the last chapter, the term *writing* was applied to a rather formal and sophisticated language activity not ever fully developed by many students, even in their first language. In contrast, when we refer to a student's skill in speaking a second language, our fundamental concern is with his ability to communicate informally on everyday subjects with sufficient ease and fluency to hold the attention of his listener. Thus in our tests of speaking ability we are primarily, if not solely, interested in the foreign student's control of the signaling systems of English—his pronunciation, grammar, and vocabulary—and not with the idea content or formal organization of the message he conveys.[1]

THE MAJOR PROBLEM IN MEASURING SPEAKING ABILITY

In earlier chapters we observed how three of the speech components—grammatical structure, vocabulary, and auditory comprehension—are now being tested by reliable and relatively simple objective techniques. It is highly probable that performance on these tests is positively related to general ability to converse in a foreign language, although, as will be explained directly, we still lack very reliable criteria for testing out this assumption.[2] General fluency, too, is fairly easy to assess, at least in gross terms: it usually takes only a few minutes of listening to determine whether a foreign speaker is able to approximate the speed and ease with which native speakers of the language typically produce their utterances.[3] It is only when we come to the crucial matter of pronunciation that we

[1] In this general discussion we can ignore those relatively rare situations in which a foreign speaker has a need to engage in formal rhetoric. On this level we would probably be dealing with a native, or near-native, level of proficiency.

[2] Experiments carried out at the American Language Institute of Georgetown University showed a correlation of .62 between the performance of 200 foreign students on a structure test and a scored interview, and a correlation of .74 between the interview ratings and the combined scores on listening and structure tests for 287 subjects.

[3] It goes without saying that the hesitation of some foreign speakers is the result of shyness—perhaps a cultural matter—rather than of inadequate command of the second language.

are confronted with a really serious problem of evaluation. The central reason is the lack of general agreement on what "good" pronunciation of a second language really means: is comprehensibility to be the sole basis of judgment, or must we demand a high degree of both phonemic and allophonic accuracy? And can we be certain that two or more native speakers will find the utterances of a foreign speaker equally comprehensible, or do some listeners decode a foreign accent with greater facility than others? Until we can agree on precisely how speech is to be judged and have determined that the judgments will have stability, we cannot put much confidence in oral ratings.

All that we can offer in this chapter, then, is a brief summary of the present state of a very imperfect art. Let us hope that future research may yet transform it into a reasonably exact science.

TYPES OF ORAL PRODUCTION TESTS

Most tests of oral production fall into one of the following categories:

1. Relatively unstructured interviews, rated on a carefully constructed scale
2. Highly structured speech samples (generally recorded), rated according to very specific criteria
3. Paper-and-pencil objective tests of pronunciation, presumably providing indirect evidence of speaking ability

Of the three, the rated interview is undoubtedly the most commonly used technique, and the one with the longest history. Paper-and-pencil tests of pronunciation have been used off and on for some years, generally in combination with other types of assessment. Highly structured speech samples, as the term will be used here, appear to be relatively recent and have not as yet won much acceptance in American testing of English as a second language.

Scored Interviews

The simplest and most frequently employed method of measuring oral proficiency is to have one or more trained raters interview each candidate separately and record their evaluations of his competence in the spoken language. Figure 2 illustrates a typical scale used with the interviews. It will be seen to consist of (1) a set of qualities to be rated and (2) a series of possible ratings. The ratings

Figure 2. Sample Oral-English Rating Sheet

Student:_____ Rater:_____ Date:_____ SCORE:_____

Pronunciation

___5. Has few traces of foreign accent.
___4. Always intelligible, though one is conscious of a definite accent.
___3. Pronunciation problems necessitate concentrated listening and occasionally lead to misunderstanding.
___2. Very hard to understand because of pronunciation problems. Must frequently be asked to repeat.
___1. Pronunciation problems so severe as to make speech virtually unintelligible.

Grammer

___5. Makes few (if any) noticeable errors of grammar or word order.
___4. Occasionally makes grammatical and/or word-order errors which do not, however, obscure meaning.
___3. Makes frequent errors of grammar and word order which occasionally obscure meaning.
___2. Grammar and word-order errors make comprehension difficult. Must often rephrase sentences and/or restrict himself to basic patterns.
___1. Errors in grammar and word order so severe as to make speech virtually unintelligible.

Vocabulary

___5. Use of vocabulary and idioms is virtually that of a native speaker.
___4. Sometimes uses inappropriate terms and/or must rephrase ideas because of lexical inadequacies.
___3. Frequently uses the wrong words; conversation somewhat limited because of inadequate vocabulary.
___2. Misuse of words and very limited vocabulary make comprehension quite difficult.
___1. Vocabulary limitations so extreme as to make conversation virtually impossible.

Fluency

___5. Speech as fluent and effortless as that of a native speaker.
___4. Speed of speech seems to be slightly affected by language problems.
___3. Speed and fluency are rather strongly affected by language problems.
___2. Usually hesitant; often forced into silence by language limitations.
___1. Speech is so halting and fragmentary as to make conversation virtually impossible.

Comprehension

___5. Appears to understand everything without difficulty.
___4. Understands nearly everything at normal speed, although occasional repetition may be necessary.
___3. Understands most of what is said at slower-than-normal speed with repetitions.
___2. Has great difficulty following what is said. Can comprehend only "social conversation" spoken slowly and with frequent repetitions.
___1. Cannot be said to understand even simple conversational English.

have numerical values—in this case, a range of 1 to 5 points[4]—each followed by a short behavioral statement. Sometimes, as a further refinement, the rated qualities are weighted to reflect the relative importance which the test maker attaches to each of the several speech components. Thus, for example, two or three times the weight given to fluency might be given to grammar.

As with other types of highly subjective measures, the great weakness of oral ratings is their tendency to have rather low reliability. No two interviews are conducted exactly alike, even by the same interviewer, and even though it may be argued that some variation is desirable, or even essential, it is clear that the *test reliability* will be adversely affected. Similarly, no interviewer can maintain exactly the same scoring standards throughout a large number of interviews, and these inevitable shifts in standards will lower the *rater reliability* of the measure. And the above differences will be even greater when it is not possible for the same interviewers to rate all the candidates. Nevertheless, positive steps can be taken to achieve a tolerable degree of reliability for the scored interview. Chief among these are (1) providing clear, precise, and mutually exclusive behavioral statements for each scale point; (2) training the raters for their tasks; and (3) pooling the judgments of at least two raters per interview. These and other procedures for improving interview testing will be dealt with in some detail at the end of the chapter.

Highly Structured Speech Samples

As indicated in our brief discussion of the test interview, interviewers tend consciously or unconsciously to set unequal tasks for the candidates and to score the performances on different bases because of the relatively limited nature of the guidelines provided. In an effort to minimize these weaknesses, some test writers have recently developed some very interesting oral-production tests which set highly structured speaking tasks. As a rule these tests are in several parts, each designed to elicit a somewhat different kind of speech sample. The stimuli may be oral (provided by live voice or on

[4]Ranges of 4 and 6 points are also frequently used, and there appears to be no conclusive evidence as to the optimum size of the scale. However, when fewer than 4 scale points are used, the total scores tend to bunch together, obscuring differences between subjects. And when 6 or more points are employed, it becomes extremely difficult to compose mutually exclusive behavioral statements for each level of the scale.

tape) or written, or both. The following item types, drawn from foreign language tests for native speakers of English, illustrate techniques which would be equally appropriate in English tests for foreign students.[5]

1. Sentence repetition. The examinee hears, and then repeats, a series of short sentences.

Scoring procedure: The rater listens to the pronunciation of two specific pronunciation points per sentence, marking whether or not each is pronounced in an acceptable way.[6]

Sentences	*Points to be rated*
1. Jack always likes good food.	Vowel contrast in *good:food*
2. We'll be gone for six weeks.	Vowel contrast in *six:weeks*
3. They've gone farther south.	Voiced-voiceless fricatives in *farther:south*

2. Reading passage. The examinee is given several minutes to read a passage silently, after which he is instructed to read it aloud at normal speed and with appropriate expression.

Scoring procedure: The rater marks two or more pronunciation points per sentence and then makes a general evaluation of the fluency of the reading.[7]

Examiner's copy of the test	*Points to be rated*
While Mr. Brown read his <u>new</u>paper,	primary stress
his wife finished packing his clo<u>thes</u>	voiced final consonant(s)
for the trip. The suitcase was al-	
ready quite fu<u>ll</u>, and she was having	vowel quality
a great deal of <u>diffi</u>culty finding	primary stress

---

[5] The items were inspired by the *MLA Foreign Language Proficiency Tests for Teachers and Advanced Students*, produced by Educational Testing Service. Rather similar devices were used by C. McCallien and A. Taylor in *Examination Tests in Oral English*, London: Longmans, Green & Co., Ltd., 1958.

[6] It need scarcely be pointed out that judgments of acceptability must be highly subjective. Thus even these testing techniques do not wholly overcome the problem of unstable scorer performance.

[7] The basic problem in evaluating speaking proficiency by the way a subject reads aloud is that oral reading may be a skill in itself: people do not necessarily read as they converse, and vice versa. The differences are apt to be most acute in matters of intonation.

room for the <u>shirts, socks, and</u>	series intonation
<u>handkerchiefs</u>. Turning to her hus-	
band, she a<u>sked</u>, "Are you sure you	consonant cluster
really want to <u>go on this trip</u>?"	intonation contour
"<u>I'm</u> sure," <u>replied Mr. Brown</u>,	intonation contour
"but how about <u>you</u>?"	stress and pitch

3. **Sentence conversion.** The examinee is instructed to convert or transform sentences in specific ways (from positive to negative, from statement to question, from present tense to past, etc.). The voice on the tape gives the sentences one at a time, the examinee supplying the conversion in the pause that follows.

Scoring procedure: The rater scores each converted sentence on the basis of whether or not it is grammatically acceptable.

4. **Sentence construction.** The voice on the tape asks the examinee to compose sentences appropriate to specific situations.

Scoring procedure: The rater scores each sentence on an acceptable-unacceptable basis.

1. "You are trying to find the post office in a strange city. Ask a policeman for directions."
2. "You have telephoned your friend Mary, but her mother answers and tells you that Mary is not at home. Ask her to leave a message for Mary to call you when she comes home."[8]

5. **Response to pictorial stimuli.** The examinee is given time to study each of a series of pictures and then briefly describes what is going on in each scene.

Scoring procedure: For each picture the rater gives a separate rating of the examinee's pronunciation, grammar, vocabulary, and fluency, using a 4- or 5-point scale.

Oral-production tests comprising the above, or similar, types of highly structured speech tasks offer considerable promise as replacements for the unstructured interview, for they greatly increase both test and scorer consistency. However, it must not be forgotten that the scoring still requires human judgments, and satisfactory

---

[8] Because of the relatively complicated nature of the directions, it would probably be best for these to be given in both oral and written form. Even then, a poor response or lack of response might conceivably indicate a reading/listening difficulty on the part of the subject.

reliability can be achieved only if the raters are carefully selected and are put through rigorous training sessions.[9] Moreover, such tests demand a great deal of time and care in preparation and usually require mechanical devices for proper administration. In short, structured speech-sample tests provide no shortcuts to effective oral testing.

Paper-and-Pencil Tests of Pronunciation

So far in this chapter we have described oral rating techniques which call for the eliciting and evaluating of samples of actual speech. For some years test writers have experimented with objective paper-and-pencil tests of pronunciation in which the subjects have merely to check responses indicating how they pronounce English vowels and consonants and how they stress words and phrases. Such tests assume (1) that what the foreign learner "hears" himself say silently is, in fact, what he says aloud, and (2) that a sufficiently broad range of pronunciation problems can be tested by this indirect method to allow us to generalize about a subject's overall control of the English sound system. Before discussing these assumptions, let us illustrate characteristic item types appearing in these paper-and-pencil pronunciation tests.

1. Rhyme words. The examinee is first presented with a test word which he is instructed to read to himself, after which he is to select the one word from among several alternatives which rhymes with the test word. (He is cautioned to make his selection according to sound rather than spelling.)

1. Could rhymes with   A. blood
                          B. food
                          C. wood

2. Plays rhymes with   A. case
                          B. raise
                          C. press

[9]In this connection the experience with the Speaking Tests of the *MLA Foreign Language Proficiency Tests* is particularly instructive. When in the summer of 1960 parallel forms of these tests were administered at the beginning and end of NDEA institutes for teachers, the post-testing showed almost as many score losses as there were gains. The reason, it was discovered, was that scorers had shifted their standards substantially in the course of scoring the many tapes. Therefore, when the tests were used again in the summers of 1961 and 1962, great care was taken during the scorer training sessions to emphasize the need for maintaining consistent scoring standards. As a result, in each of these two years a proportionately smaller number of institutes showed more losses than gains on the second testing, and by 1962 the correlation between the scores given by two scorers for each tape was found to be .89—very respectable reliability for a test involving individual scorer judgments. (See *A Study of Pre- and Post-test Results in the 1962 NDEA Summer Foreign Language Institutes*, TDR 62.3, Princeton, N.J.: Educational Testing Service, 1962.)

2. Word stress. The examinee is to decide which syllable in each test word receives the heaviest stress.

```
                1. frequently
                   1   2  3
                2. introduce
                   1  2  3
                3. develop
                   1 2 3
```

3. Phrase stress. The examinee is to decide which one of several numbered syllables in each utterance would receive the heaviest stress.

```
1. I know that Henry went to the movie, but where did John go?
                              1     2     3    4     5
2. I'm certain Professor Brown wants to see you, but he's in class just now.
                                                   1    2    3     4    5
```

To have confidence in such paper-and-pencil tests of speaking ability, we would need strong statistical evidence of their validity, that is, evidence that they are really testing what they purport to test. How accurate *are* a subject's impressions of how he speaks? And does he pronounce words and phrases silently in exactly the same way that he pronounces them aloud? To answer such questions we would need some trustworthy external criterion—some reliable measure of how the subjects actually do speak—and, as already noted, it is the lack of such a measure that is still the chief stumbling block to all our efforts to evaluate oral production with real precision. Testing specialists who have used the paper-and-pencil objective tests have attempted to validate them by comparing test results with judges' evaluations of the subjects' oral reading of the test items. That such experiments have yielded conflicting results should not surprise us, particularly inasmuch as some of the experimenters specifically reported a serious lack of rater agreement on the oral readings.

If, however, we have been unable to establish either the validity or the invalidity of these tests by rigorous statistical methods, we can cite a number of observations which cast considerable doubt on their efficacy. In the first place, the users of such tests have frequently observed that some students with superior pronunciation have done poorly on the tests, while high scores have sometimes been obtained by students who could barely be understood. Such experiences would suggest a possible deficiency in the test method.

Secondly, one cannot help wondering about the technique of testing the production of the segmental phonemes by means of rhyme items. There is certainly no guarantee that just because a speaker pronounces two words alike he is pronouncing them correctly: he may be replacing the correct English phoneme with another English phoneme, or distorting the correct phoneme to the point where most native speakers would have trouble comprehending.

Thirdly, even a casual examination of the range of problems treated in these tests inspires the strongest suspicions that they sample the total sound system most inadequately. Rhyme items cannot test sounds in word-initial position; they take no account of the assimilations and other phenomena of normal connected discourse; and they are largely ineffective in testing the consonants (and some vowels) where spelling in most cases is a dead giveaway.[10] Similarly, the tests of phrase stress and intonation are of necessity most superficial, leaving untouched most of the really significant matters of pitch contour to which the good teacher of English as a second language devotes so many hours of instruction and drill.

Summary

The foregoing discussion of oral testing techniques may be summarized as follows:

1. The validity of paper-and-pencil objective techniques remains largely unproven; such techniques should therefore be used with caution, and certainly never as the sole measure of oral proficiency.

2. The technique of eliciting and rating highly structured speech samples shows much promise, but such testing is still in the experimental stage and requires very great test-writing skill and experience.

3. The scored interview, though not so reliable a measure as we would wish for, is still probably the best technique for use in relatively informal, small-scale testing situations; and ways can be

---

[10]Because of these limitations, most tests of this type show one or another of the following weaknesses: (1) certain sound contrasts are overtested and others are neglected; (2) problems are filled out with nonfunctioning distracters; (3) infrequent lexical items are included in the choices so that the problems are in part tests of vocabulary.

shown for substantially improving the effectiveness of this testing device.

Following the third point, we shall conclude this chapter with a consideration of some of the ways to improve interview ratings.

IMPROVING THE SCORED INTERVIEW

General Procedures

1. Decide in advance on interview methods and rating standards. Prior to interviewing, the raters should meet together to discuss and agree upon the general method of conducting the interviews and the specific bases for scoring. For unless the raters all follow the same general procedures (by devoting approximately the same length of time to the average interview, speaking to the candidates at about the same rate of speed, maintaining the same level of difficulty in the questions they ask) and apply the same general rating standards, the results will be neither reliable nor valid. An extremely useful device is to play recordings of previous interviews and have the raters score these. By then discussing both the interview techniques and the scoring, the raters should be able to reach basic agreement on methods and standards, thereby ensuring a reasonable degree of uniformity.

2. Conduct the interviews in some quiet place with suitable acoustics. Echoes, street noises, conversation in an adjacent room, and the like, will naturally impose an unfair burden on the candidates and greatly reduce the reliability and validity of the ratings.

3. Reserve sufficient time for each interview. In general, ten to fifteen minutes would seem essential as the minimum for each interview, though the time required will vary somewhat from candidate to candidate. (We shall return to this point in the suggestions for conducting the interview.)

4. Use at least two raters for each candidate. At least two independent ratings are necessary if satisfactory rater reliability is to be obtained. The two (or more) raters may either interview separately, one after the other in different rooms, or they may independently score the same performance. If the latter system is used, it is generally advisable for one of the raters to conduct the interview while the other observes (and later scores) from the back of the room. What should be avoided is giving the candidate the impression that he is appearing before a panel of judges, for in such a situation the natural shyness of some candidates will affect the performance.

5. Rate the candidates without reference to other test scores. Sound testing practice requires that precautions be taken against possible scorer bias. Therefore, candidates' scores on other tests should be withheld from the raters until after they have completed their evaluations.

6. Record the ratings after the interview. No effort should be made to score a candidate during his interview, for this will tend to upset him and will certainly make him acutely conscious of the testing nature of the interview. It is enough if the interviewer simply puts down the candidate's name and other necessary routine data, preferably on a plain pad of paper. Actual scoring should be done immediately after the candidate leaves the room, and therefore the procedure for bringing in the candidates should be so arranged that the next examinee will not enter until the marking has been completed.

7. Obtain each candidate's final score by pooling or averaging the two (or more) ratings that have been given him. If the difference between the ratings is clearly excessive, the candidate should be called back for a second evaluation.

Suggestions for Conducting the Interviews

1. Beginning the interview. The interview should begin with a few minutes of social questions: "How are you today?" "What city do you come from?" "How long have you studied English?" "What do you plan to do when you finish your studies?" Such questioning will serve the double purpose of helping to put the candidate at ease and of determining how well he can function in a social situation.

During the initial period the interviewer should speak at normal conversational speed. If it is immediately apparent that the candidate cannot comprehend what is being said to him, it may be necessary for the interviewer to modify his speech somewhat, speaking more slowly and with some simplification of sentence structure and vocabulary—while making a mental note to score the candidate accordingly. If the candidate continues to have extreme difficulty, it is best to make the interview brief—though pleasant. It is valueless to attempt to carry on a prolonged interview in what can easily degenerate into non-English on the part of both participants.

2. Continuing the interview. After the routine preliminary questions, the interviewer should move on to other areas of discussion and follow lines of questioning which the examinee has not been able to anticipate. Questioning should reveal the candidate's proficiency in handling the kinds of subject matter that will be required of him in the classroom.[11]

Varying the line of questioning with each of a large number of candidates is admittedly rather difficult. With practice, however, it can be done, and it is absolutely essential that the questioning should not always follow a set pattern. (Most veteran interviewers are familiar with the candidate who immediately launches into a prepared speech on a subject for which the previous interviewees have obviously prepared him.)

Although an interview is generally thought of as questioning by one party and answering by the other, the kind of aural/oral testing now under consideration calls for some additional techniques. It would be well for the interviewer occasionally to interject his own ideas on the subject being discussed, thus permitting him to observe how well the candidate can comprehend, and respond to, expository speech. (Of course it goes without saying that this technique should not be overdone, with the candidate ultimately becoming a mute listener.)

3. Concluding the interview. When the interviewer is satisfied that he can make an accurate appraisal of the candidate's English proficiency, the interview should be brought courteously to an end. Whatever the precise form that the conclusion takes, care should be taken not to give the candidate the impression that he is being cut off in the middle of a discussion. Instead, he should be left with the feeling that the interview was a pleasant experience for both him and the interviewer.

---

[11] One cannot, however, approve of the rather common practice of giving the examinee a book in his field, asking him to read a page, and then discussing the contents with him. Clearly this is mixing two kinds of tests, reading and speaking, and it would be extremely difficult to know whether a poor performance indicated poor reading comprehension or poor oral production.

 *Constructing*

the Test

The construction of an educational test includes the following steps:

1. Planning the test
2. Preparing the test items and directions
3. Submitting the test material to review and revising on the basis of review
4. Pretesting the material and analyzing the results
5. Assembling the final form of the test
6. Reproducing the test

In this chapter we shall briefly describe each step in the process of test construction as applied to the testing of English as a second language. Our treatment of step 2, the most important and time-consuming part of the process, will be confined to a few points not fully covered in the previous chapters.

PLANNING THE TEST

Effective testing requires careful planning. Yet as reasonable and obvious as that statement may sound, all too many educational measures—and particularly those prepared by classroom teachers—are constructed without sufficient forethought. It is just too easy for the amateur test writer to take pen in hand and turn out items without much consideration of the balance or adequacy of the resulting test content. Except by chance, such a test will not prove a very valid measure of the specific skills that the testing situation calls for.

The following steps provide a brief guide to the planning of tests of English as a second language. We have arbitrarily chosen to describe the planning of a final achievement test in a hypothetical course of study. Very similar procedures would be followed in the planning of a general proficiency test, except that the test outline would have to be built on a broader base than simply the content of a single course. Probably in this case the test writer would wish to seek the advice of a panel of subject-matter experts or analyze the content of a cross section of widely used and well-regarded textbooks to establish the topics of his test outline and the emphasis to be given to each.

Step 1: Determining the General Course Objectives

In the preparation of an achievement test, one may base the test objectives directly on the objectives of the course. Sometimes such objectives have been carefully formulated by the teacher or his department, and in other cases they are implicit in the methods and materials of the course. Let us suppose, for example, that our task is to prepare a final examination in an intensive intermediate-level course in English as a second language for secondary-school students. We find that the course content is as follows:

1. Textbook lessons, each consisting of
   a. Short reading selection (simple description or exposition)
   b. Dialogue
   c. Pronunciation drill
   d. Grammar drill
   e. Word study
   f. Homework grammar exercise
2. Laboratory practice, including drill on dialogue and pronunciation points keyed to the textbook

3. Weekly compositions based on topics related to the textbook readings

From the course coverage it is clear that the general objectives of the course are:

1. To increase skill in listening comprehension
2. To increase skill in oral production
3. To develop skill in reading simple descriptive and expository prose
4. To develop skill in writing simple description and exposition

Our basic objectives, then, are to measure the extent to which students have acquired or improved their control of these skills.

Step 2: Dividing the General Course Objectives into Their Components

The objectives we defined in step 1 were extremely broad. As our next step, then, we need to break them down into their specific components, after which we may determine which of these components we shall measure in our final examination.

In Chapter 1 it was suggested that listening, speaking, reading, and writing each include four elements:

1. **Phonology/orthography**: the sound system (in listening and speaking) and graphic system (in reading and writing), which seem sufficiently parallel to be treated in a test outline as a single "either-or" component of language.
2. **Grammatical structure**: the system of grammatical signaling devices. Not all grammatical patterns are equally common in the written and spoken forms of the language. Many, however, are; and it is probable that in our intermediate-level materials use is made of structure points that are equally appropriate in the exercise of all four skills.
3. **Vocabulary**: the lexical items needed to function effectively in each of the four skills. The advanced-level learner of a language has several "word stocks": (*a*) the items that he uses in speech but not in writing, and vice versa; (*b*) words that he recognizes in listening and/or reading but does not himself employ in his speaking and writing. Such differences are probably not great at the intermediate level of instruction,

however. We may assume that the course materials utilize much the same stock of lexical items in the reading selections, dialogues, and writing exercises—that the various types of activities are designed to reinforce the learning of a controlled vocabulary.

4. **Rate and general fluency**: the speed and ease with which the user of a language can decode and encode messages. In intermediate-level courses we ordinarily put a good deal of time and effort into increasing students' aural/oral facility but do not concern ourselves much with the sheer rate of reading and writing—linguistic activities that are perhaps being introduced (as skills in themselves) for the first time and where, therefore, the emphasis is simply on developing the students' control of the basic signaling devices.

Step 3: Establishing the General Design of the Test

Our two preliminary steps have established the objectives of our hypothetical course in sufficient detail to enable us now to decide upon the general design of the final achievement test. At this point two extremely important factors must be considered: the time to be provided for testing, and the degree of speededness we wish to build into our test.

Let us assume that a maximum of two hours has been scheduled for the final examination. Of the total 120 minutes, we should reserve *at least* 10 minutes for administrative procedures: seating the students and handing out the materials, giving general directions, collecting the materials at the end of the testing period, handling unanticipated problems, etc. We are thus left with 110 minutes for actual testing.

The issue of whether or not tests of English as a second language should be highly speeded is somewhat complex. As already noted in this book, speed of performance is unquestionably an important aspect of language proficiency. On the other hand, slow *test* performance may be due to the foreign students' unfamiliarity with certain test techniques (particularly the multiple-choice types) which are relatively uncommon in many parts of the world, where examinations may still consist of fairly leisurely grammar-translation exercises. It would probably be fairest and safest in most common testing situations (e.g., in general screening tests or final examinations in English courses) to time the tests so that all but the slowest 10 or 15 percent of the subjects—those most likely to have severe rate-of-performance problems—are able to attempt all the items. Such a compromise should not seriously impair the validity of our test for foreign students, and it may quite possibly increase the reliability of the measure. Let us agree, then, to provide fairly liberal time allotments for the achievement test we shall now begin to design.

Our earlier determination of course components would suggest that two parts of the test should be devoted to *structure* and *vocabulary*, two basic components of all four skills taught in the course. For each of these parts we should make immediate decisions about the type and number of items, bearing in mind our overall limit of 110 minutes for testing. Because our test will be administered to a rather small number of examinees and can be scored more or less at leisure, we can safely use supply types of items for at least some portions of our test. As we noted in earlier chapters, supply (short-answer) items require less preparation time and somewhat less test-writing proficiency than multiple-choice items and would therefore be appropriate for the kind of teacher-made test we are considering.

In our chapter on the testing of structure, we observed that the fill-in item type is particularly useful in informal classroom situations.[1] Such items require the examinee to complete or rewrite sentences in a prescribed manner. Although the time required to complete these items will vary somewhat according to the complexity of the tasks, we may suppose that in general the reasonably proficient student can answer fill-in problems at the rate of about 1 1/2 per minute, including time for the reading of the directions and the mental adjustment that will accompany each new section (for we must assume that the various types of structure problems will have to be grouped into several sections). Reasonable test coverage can probably be achieved with 70 structure items, for which we shall allow forty-five minutes.

For the vocabulary part of our test, we may use the supply item type termed the paraphrase in our chapter on the testing of vocabulary.[2] This item type, it will be remembered, consists of a

---

[1] See p. 29 above.
[2] See p. 53 above.

sentence with an underlined test word; the examinee is to rewrite the sentence, substituting other words for the underlined portion. Such items go quite slowly; we shall have to allow about one minute per item. Let us plan on 40 items to be answered in another forty-five-minute period.

Including the time reserved for administrative procedures, we have now accounted for 100 of our allotted 120 minutes, and so far we have made no provision for the testing of *phonology*, which is clearly an important component of our course. As we observed in earlier chapters, the testing of listening ability is relatively easy, while in contrast the testing of oral production is both difficult and inexact. For our teacher-made test, therefore, it would be prudent to settle for an objective measure of sound discrimination and general auditory comprehension. The two sections might be planned as follows:

Section One: Sound Discrimination. The examinee hears sets of three words and is asked to indicate which two are the same. Twenty items.

Section Two: Auditory Comprehension. The examinee hears a series of questions and for each question indicates which one of four printed choices would make a logical answer.[3] Twenty items.

The 40-item objective test outlined above can be administered easily in twenty minutes.

Our test outline is now complete:

Part	Item type	Number of items	Minutes
1. Listening	Multiple-choice	40	20
2. Structure	Short-answer	70	45
3. Vocabulary	Short-answer	40	45
		150	110
		Administration:	10
			120

[3]For a further description of these two item types, see pp. 33 and 36-37 above.

We should now check our test content against the detailed course outline we prepared earlier. Figure 3 plots the test content on a grid showing the principal components of the four skills areas of the course. The checkmarks indicate the components which our proposed test will measure. As we see from the chart, our test measures most of the goals of instruction; we would not suppose that this or any other single test could measure *all* the objectives that the teacher has tried to achieve. Quite probably the teacher would add other criteria to the final examination in making his final evaluation of the students. For example, we noted earlier in our description of the

Figure 3. The Components of an Intermediate-level ESL Course
Used as a Checklist for the Design of the Final Examination

Components	Language Skills			
	Listening	Speaking	Reading	Writing
Phonology/ortho-graphy	√			
Structure	√	√	√	√
Vocabulary	√	√	√	√
Rate and general fluency	√		/////	/////

Check marks indicate components measured by the final examination.
Shaded areas indicate components not emphasized in the course.

course content that there were weekly compositions, and the teacher would almost surely wish to include the scores or grades on these in his final evaluation of student achievement. In addition it would be possible to give a general rating of the student's progress in oral production on the basis of his daily class performance.

The next step in the construction of our test would be the selection of the specific problems on which to base our test items. As we have emphasized throughout the book, the content of an achievement test should directly reflect the course content. Our procedure would therefore be to prepare an inventory of the phonological points, grammatical structures, and lexical items treated in the class textbook and to make a note of the emphasis given to each. Quite probably we would find that our list contained more items than we could possibly cover in a two-hour examination, and some types of problems would have to be eliminated. As a starting point, we might feel justified in omitting some of the material from the earlier chapters if it were clearly a review of what our students had mastered at a previous stage of learning. We could thus concentrate on those matters that were new to most of the students when introduced during the course of our instruction. But even then we might be left with more problem types than could be included in 150 test items. We might then proceed to reduce our list on the basis of our answers to the following questions:

1. Which phonemic contrasts presented major difficulties to our students?
2. Which grammatical structures received the most emphasis in the course and required continued review?
3. Which vocabulary items would seem to have the greatest utility value to our students?

If some decisions about test content proved especially difficult, we could at least console ourselves by remembering that *all educational testing is a sampling process* and that our final examination would probably be only one of several measures that would be taken into account in our final evaluation.

With these remarks we shall leave our consideration of what might go into one specific examination and return to the discussion of general principles of test construction.

PREPARING THE TEST ITEMS AND DIRECTIONS

Additional Notes on the Preparation of Items

In the preparation of multiple-choice or short-answer (supply) items, it is always necessary to write more items than will be needed in the final form of the test. In the first place, a careful review of the complete collection of items will almost surely disclose flaws in individual items that were not apparent at the time of writing, and some material will therefore have to be discarded. Secondly, if the material is submitted to a full-fledged pretesting, still more items will be found inappropriate or defective, and a further reduction will be necessary. It is never possible to predict exactly what proportion of the original items will survive item review and pretesting; however, a reasonable rule of thumb is to begin with at least 30 to 40 percent more material than will finally be required. To ensure that the reduction of items does not leave important problems untested in the final form, one may wish to begin with two or three items testing the same general point. Very often one such item will do well in pretesting while another will, for any of a variety of reasons, prove ineffective.

As items are written, it is a good procedure to type each one on a separate slip of paper (5- by 8-inch size is recommended), with the answer on the back. Slips are much more convenient to work with than sheets: items can easily be added or deleted, and the material can be reordered without the necessity of recopying. The answer should be put on the back of the slip so that an outside reviewer will not be influenced before he makes his own decision as to the correct response.

Writing Test Directions

Test directions should be brief, simple to understand, and free from possible ambiguities. They should be accompanied by sufficient examples to ensure that even the slow learner or least skilled examinee understands the problem type. Clear instructions on whether or not examinees are to guess at answers should be provided.[4] It is usually advisable, too, to indicate the length of time which will be allowed for the test or its several parts. If the test is highly speeded, examinees should be prepared for this in the directions so that they will not become unnerved by their inability to finish.

In short, the purpose of test directions is to allow all examinees to begin the problems on an equal footing. If the language of the directions is difficult or confusing, one cannot be sure that poor test

---

[4] The question of the effect of guessing will be discussed in Chap. 11.

performance indicates low proficiency in the skills area being tested. If the number or the explanation of the examples is inadequate, what was designed as a proficiency or achievement test may become partly an intelligence test instead. Note the following:

> ... final punctuation has been omitted to eliminate orthographic clues to the answers.

It is doubtful whether this "explanation," taken from the directions to an English test for foreigners, will be understood by more than a small portion of the examinees. The others may quite possibly waste valuable time trying to puzzle out the meaning of such language and, failing in their efforts, become unduly anxious and upset over their failure.

REVIEWING THE ITEMS

When the items have all been written, they should be set aside for a few days before being reviewed by the writer. Once he is satisfied with his material, it should be submitted to at least one colleague with experience in the subject-matter field—as, in this case, a teacher of English as a second language. Comments by the outside reviewer can be put on the back of the item slips; items judged satisfactory can be marked "O.K." with the reviewer's initials. Careful review will often identify items which otherwise would be lost later in pretesting or would arouse the criticism of the subject-matter specialists were they to appear in the final version of the test. Very often minor defects in items can be corrected and the items salvaged.

PRETESTING THE MATERIAL

Standard objective tests consist of pretested materials. That is to say, all the items have first been tried out on a fairly large number of subjects of the same kind as those for whom the test is being designed. Only those items which prove statistically satisfactory in the pretest are included in the final version of the test. Items are said to be statistically satisfactory if they meet two requirements:

1. If they are of a suitable level of difficulty—neither too hard nor too easy for the population being tested

2. If they discriminate between those examinees who know the material or have the skills or abilities being tested, and those who do not

Pretesting also provides an opportunity for the test maker to try out the test directions and to check the estimated time required for examinees to work the items of the test. If the directions are not clear to the subjects, this should certainly be noted at the time of pretesting so that the instructions can be clarified in the final form. If a large number of subjects are unable to answer items at the anticipated rate of speed, the test maker may wish to reduce the number of items or increase the time allowance on the final form of the test.

Effective pretesting requires, above all, that the pretest subjects be as similar as possible to the kind of examinees for whom the final form of the test is intended. The closer the two groups are to each other, the more meaningful will be the pretest data. In addition, however, some test writers like to administer their tests of English as a second language to a sample of native speakers of English as a form of item validation: items which cause difficulty for subjects who use English natively perhaps do not belong in a test for foreign learners. (As we have noted in earlier chapters, however, this principle would not necessarily apply to some kinds of advanced-level tests, such as those of reading comprehension or writing ability, which are skills in which native speakers of English show a wide range of ability.)

A second important point in pretesting is to allow sufficient time for all, or nearly all, examinees to attempt every item, for if a substantial number do not reach the end of the pretest, there will be insufficient data on the last items in the pretest. It is common, therefore, to allow more generous time limits for pretests than for the final form of a test. If the test writer needs to determine the speed at which most subjects can work the problems, he can call time at an appropriate point in the pretest and have the subjects mark the item they have reached. Those who have not completed the test can then be allowed to proceed to the end.

In the case of informal classroom tests, pretesting is seldom practicable, and in the preparation of such tests this step, and item analysis, may need to be omitted.[5] Pretesting is, however, essential

[5] Even with these tests, however, item analysis conducted after the testing is useful in determining which items worked most effectively; these may be put into an "item pool" for reuse at a later date.

for any test that is to be administered to large numbers of examinees and used to make important decisions about these subjects—as, for instance, a test designed to screen university applicants or to place such students in appropriate classes.

ANALYZING THE PRETEST RESULTS (ITEM ANALYSIS)

After the pretest answer sheets have been accumulated (and there should be a safe number of these—generally at least 100 completed papers), the items should be analyzed to determine their effectiveness in terms of the two criteria listed in the preceding section.

Determining Item Difficulty

The first step is to determine the difficulty level of each item. Though much more sophisticated techniques have been developed, a very satisfactory method is simply to ascertain the percent of the sample who answered each item correctly. Multiple-choice items that are excessively easy (say, those correctly answered by at least 92 percent of the examinees) or unreasonably difficult (perhaps those answered correctly by less than 30 percent of the sample group) will generally be discarded as not contributing significantly to the measurement function of the test.[6] Those which remain must still meet the second of the two requirements, that is, discrimination.

Determining Item Discrimination

The second step, then, is to determine how well each item discriminates between high- and low-level examinees, for each item in a test should help to separate the proficient subjects from those who lack the tested skills or learnings.

[6] There will occasionally be exceptions. For instance, if a test is of a highly unusual nature, it may be felt desirable to begin with several "giveaway" items—those which are exceptionally easy—in order to start all the candidates out on the right track. The same results, however, may be achieved more efficiently by including a sufficient number of sample items, and it is usually preferable to include in the actual test only items which make a real contribution to the measure.

The usual method is to assume that an examinee's performance on the total test will provide a reasonably good indication of his level of achievement or proficiency. Therefore, the test analyst will first separate the highest and lowest papers in terms of the total scores on the test. He will then determine how the two groups did on each item; the discriminating items will be those answered correctly by more of the high group than the low group.

Of the several statistical techniques that have been devised for calculating item discrimination, the following is one of the simpler methods that can be recommended to the classroom teacher.[7]

Step 1. Separate the highest and the lowest 25 percent of the papers.

Step 2. For each item, subtract the number of "lows" who answered the item correctly from the number of "highs" who answered correctly. (If more "lows" that "highs" get an item right, the result of this calculation will of course be negative and should be marked with a minus sign.)

Step 3. Divide the result of step 2 by the number of papers in each group, "highs" and "lows," to obtain the "item discrimination index."

For example, if one has a sample of 100 completed papers, he should separate the highest and the lowest 25 papers. Let us then say that the first item was answered correctly by 22 "highs" and 10 "lows." Subtracting 10 from 22, we obtain +12, which, divided by 25 (the size of each group of papers), gives an item discrimination index of +.48. We would conclude that this item has satisfactory discriminating power. Items showing negative discrimination or low discrimination (discrimination much below .30) should be either revised or discarded.

---

[7]Other techniques are described in the standard texts on educational measurement. Frequently these are based on the analysis of the top and bottom 27 percent of the papers, the proportion found most effective in determining the discriminative power of an item. Some techniques make use of conversion tables such as the familiar one developed by J. C. Flanagan to obtain a "normalized biserial coefficient of correlation" between the performance of the "highs" and "lows." (Such a table will be found in Henry E. Garrett, *Statistics in Psychology and Education*, 5th ed. New York, London, and Toronto: Longmans, Green & Co., 1958, p. 366.)

Determining the Effectiveness of Distracters

One further step in the analysis of multiple-choice items is highly desirable, and that is to inspect the way each item distracter functioned. If an item contains a distracter which attracted no one, not even the poorest examinees, it is a nonfunctioning choice which will increase the chances that some examinees will get the item right by guessing between or among the remaining two or three possibilities. Again, an inspection of the performance of distracters will sometimes show that a "wrong" answer attracted more high than low scorers. Retaining such a distracter will actually harm the test. Nonfunctioning and malfunctioning distracters should be replaced, but the revised items should then be pretested again, for the original statistics will almost always be affected by alterations.

Recording Item Analysis Data

It is most convenient to record item analysis data on an "item analysis slip" which contains (1) the item, written out in full, (2) an identification of the pretest in which the item was tried out, (3) the position of the item in the pretest, (4) the item difficulty and discrimination indices, and, in the case of multiple-choice items, (5) a tabulation of how the "highs" and "lows" responded to the several choices. (Some test writers like to include the performance of the "mid" group of examinees as well.) A sample item analysis slip is shown in Figure 4.

Figure 4. Sample Item Analysis Slip

Pretest _X-B (vocab)_

Item No. _40_

a brief, light sleep

A. yawn   C. nap
B. stroll   D. hug

Choices	Highs	Mids	Lows	
A	1	4	5	Difficulty: _.66_
B	2	6	5	Discrimination: _.48_
C	22	34	10	
D	0	4	4	
Omit	0	2	1	

The use of item analysis slips will greatly simplify the preparation of the final form of a test, for they are easy to work with during the assembly of the test and need merely be reordered to provide the material for the typist.

ASSEMBLING THE FINAL FORM

On the basis of pretesting, any necessary changes in the directions can be effected, and the selection of usable items can be made. In part the choice of items will depend upon the overall level of difficulty desired. In most testing situations it is advisable to begin with rather easy items, lead gradually to more difficult problems, and end with those items which only the best candidates can answer correctly. For a language test intended to discriminate well at various levels of competence, a wide range of item difficulty with a mean between 60 and 70 percent is recommended. Such a test will challenge most of the students yet will not include many items so difficult as to discourage large numbers of the less proficient subjects.

In assembling multiple-choice items in the final form, the test maker must take care not only to order the items according to increasing level of difficulty but also to ensure that (1) each answer position is used about the same number of times and (2) the answer positions do not form any observable pattern. For example, if we have a test consisting of one hundred 4-choice items, each answer position, A, B, C, and D, should occur about twenty-five times, the answers having the appearance of a completely random sequence (BDACDBAACBDCADA, etc.)

REPRODUCING THE TEST

1. It is essential that test materials be reproduced as clearly as possible, for poor reproduction of a test will almost certainly affect student performance. For large-scale testing, photo-offset or letter-press printing is customary; such methods provide the sharpest text and also the greatest number of good copies. For local, small-scale tests, duplication may be by mimeograph, multilith, or a similar process. Ditto (spirit carbon) processes are the least satisfactory, both because the copies often lack clarity and because only a limited number of copies can be made per master.

2. Test material should be spaced so as to provide maximum readability. With most multiple-choice item types, two columns per page will make the reading task easiest. On the other hand, with short-answer (supply) items it is generally best to extend the text the full width of the paper.

3. No multiple-choice item should be begun on one page and continued on the next, for such a break in the text will disrupt the reader's train of thought.

4. When blanks are left for the completion of short-answer items, a guideline should be provided on which the examinee may write his response. Guidelines should be of sufficient length that even the examinees with large handwriting will not have to crowd their answers.

5. It is advisable to indicate at the bottom of each page whether the examinee is to continue on to the next page or stop his work. In the former case, a simple instruction such as "Continue on the next page" should be given. If each part of the test is separately timed, the last item in each part should be followed by instructions such as: "STOP. Do not go on to the next part of the test until you are told to do so. If you finish this part before time is called, you may check your work on this part only."

6. If each part of the test is separately timed, the directions for each part should occupy a right-hand page of the book so that examinees cannot see the next set of items until the examiner gives instructions to turn the page.

7. The use of a separate cover sheet will prevent examinees from looking at the test material before the actual administration begins. If the responses are to be made in the test book, the cover sheet can include spaces for the examinee's name, class, the date, etc. The cover sheet is also the best place for giving general information and instructions about the test, such as:

   a. The general purpose of the test
   b. The method of recording responses
   c. The method of changing answers if the examinee changes his mind
   d. Information on whether or not guessing is penalized
   e. In the case of reusable test books, an admonition not to write in the book

8. The pages of the test book should be stapled together with

great care so that the back pages will not become detached in the course of handling. Moreover, the staples should be so placed that the book can be opened wide enough for the text on the stapled side of the pages to be read with ease.

USING SEPARATE ANSWER SHEETS FOR MULTIPLE-CHOICE TESTS

In large testing programs where the scoring of multiple-choice tests is done by machines, the use of separate answer sheets is mandatory. But even when the tests are hand scored, it is usually economical to have answers recorded on separate answer sheets rather than in the test books themselves. Not only may the books then be used again, but a great deal of time will be saved in scoring, for the various types of keys can be applied much more easily to single-page answer sheets than to test books.

It must be remembered, however, that separate answer sheets always complicate the mechanics of test-taking, and particularly so in the case of foreign examinees, who quite likely have had little or no previous experience with such devices. The most serious dangers are two in number: (1) that the examinee will not understand how the answer sheet is to be used; (2) that he will lose his place on the answer sheet and record his answers on the wrong lines.

The first danger may best be avoided, or at least substantially reduced, by including examples of correctly marked answers on the answer sheet and referring to these in the general test directions:[8]

. . .and thus the answer to Example Number 1 is choice A. Look on your answer sheet and see how choice A has been marked for you.

It is also advisable for the examiners to circulate among the examinees at the commencement of the test to see that each one is marking his answers in the proper way.

The danger of the examinee's losing his place is a more difficult one to eliminate, and even the most practiced test-taker occasionally makes errors of this sort. One form of help is the use of letters rather than numbers to indicate choices:

[8] Another related technique is to have the examinees do a number of sample problems themselves, which the examiners should then check on.

3. affluent

A. quick
B. sharp
C. noisy
D. wealthy

It will be easier for the examinee to remember and mark 3-D as his answer than 3-4, which might get reversed in the recording process. Sometimes this device is carried one step further and alternating sets of letters are used with the choices; thus odd-numbered items might have A, B, C, D for the choices, and even-numbered items have E, F, G, H, thereby reducing the possibility of an examinee's skipping one line on the answer sheet and consequently mis-keying the rest of his answers.

Figure 5 shows part of a homemade answer sheet which can be used in local testing. Special long-handled hole punches can be purchased for the preparation of a *stencil key* for such answer sheets. The key is made by first marking the correct answers on an answer sheet and then punching out these correct responses. When the key is placed over an examinee's answer sheet, only his correct responses will appear, and the scorer can make a mark with a colored pencil in the holes which contain no response. By counting up the colored marks, the scorer obtains the number of incorrect items and omits.

If the proper kind of punch is not available, one can prepare a *fan* or *accordion key*, which is simply a correctly marked answer sheet folded so that each vertical column of keyed answers can be placed directly beside the same column on the examinee's answer sheet.

Figure 5. Part of a Homemade Answer Sheet

Score_____

Vocabulary Test for Students of English as a Second Language

Name _____ Date_____

Native language_____ Country_____

1. ( ) ( ) ( ) ( ) A B C D	21. ( ) ( ) ( ) ( ) A B C D	41. ( ) ( ) ( ) ( ) A B C D
2. ( ) ( ) ( ) ( ) A B C D	22. ( ) ( ) ( ) ( ) A B C D	42. ( ) ( ) ( ) ( ) A B C D
3. ( ) ( ) ( ) ( ) A B C D	23. ( ) ( ) ( ) ( ) A B C D	43. ( ) ( ) ( ) ( ) A B C D
4. ( ) ( ) ( ) ( ) A B C D	24. ( ) ( ) ( ) ( ) A B C D	44. ( ) ( ) ( ) ( ) A B C D

PREPARING EQUIVALENT FORMS

It is sometimes advisable to prepare more than one form of a test that is going to be used repeatedly. *Equivalent*, or *parallel*, forms are useful for a number of purposes, of which the following are the most common.

1. **To provide for pre- and post-testing.**   One form may be used at at the beginning of a course of study or training program, and another form at the conclusion of the program to determine degree of improvement. It is better to use two equivalent forms for this purpose than to repeat the same form, for some examinees may remember specific item content.

2. **To decrease the chance of "test compromise."**   Two or more forms of a test, administered alternately according to an irregular schedule, will help reduce the temptation on the part of examinees to memorize test content and pass it on to their friends.

By far the simplest way to construct equivalent forms is to pretest sufficient material to assemble two forms on the basis of a single item analysis. The two forms should have similar item-difficulty distributions and follow the same *general* content-area specifications. Thus, for example, both forms of a structure test should have the same number of items testing word order, tense of verbs, etc. The *specific* content of the items in the two forms, however, should be different so as to constitute two samplings of word-order problems, verb-tense problems, etc.

Constructing two or more forms of a test simultaneously of course requires a good deal of pretesting: if a final form of 70 items is required, one will have to prepare and pretest a minimum of about 180 items (70 X 2 + 30 percent extra to allow accurate matching and to compensate for pretest item casualties). The best procedure would be to organize the material into two 90-item pretests and to administer these to the same pretest group(s) on two days within the same week. Where practicable, the pretests should be administered in opposite order to the two halves of the pretest population in order to neutralize the "practice effect."

Once the two forms have been prepared, it is important to try them out on other examinees to ensure that the forms really are equivalent in difficulty, for the difficulty of individual items may change when they are moved to different positions in the tests.

There are also statistical methods for preparing a second form of a test after the first form has been in use for some time, but these techniques are considerably more complicated.[9]

[9]For a discussion of procedures for constructing equivalent forms or obtaining equivalent test scores, see John C. Flanagan, "Units, Scores, and Norms," in E. F. Lindquist (ed.), *Educational Measurement*, Washington: American Council on Education, 1951, pp. 749-760.

10 *Administering the Test*

Both the reliability and the validity of a test are highly dependent on the manner in which the instrument is employed. Improper administrations can cause entire groups to perform at less than their maximum effectiveness and thus invalidate intergroup comparisons. Or such administrations can impair the performance of individual examinees and thus cause them to compare poorly with the rest of the group because of factors outside the test itself. A "perfect" test administration would be one that allowed all examinees to perform at their best under identical conditions. While perhaps this ideal is seldom attained, every effort should certainly be made to come as close to it as possible.

Most good standard tests include fairly detailed instructions for examiners or testing supervisors, usually in the form of a separate manual. Where these are provided, they should of course be followed to the letter. If such instructions are not available, or if the teacher is preparing his own test, the following outline may prove useful.[1]

---

[1] Although these suggestions are designed primarily for large-scale testing, many can be applied by the teacher in his informal classroom testing as well.

PREPARING FOR THE TEST

A smooth test administration depends in large part on thorough preparations. These are largely the responsibility of the examiner or test supervisor and should include the following steps.

1. **Selecting the testing room.** Testing must be conducted in a quiet, well-lighted room located where there will be a minimum of outside noise and interference. Care must be taken to ensure that no other group has reserved the testing room for the period of the test administration. The testing room should be large enough to permit the seating of examinees at a reasonable distance from one another (see below), but, on the other hand, it should not be so large that examinees cannot hear directions clearly or the proctors cannot keep watch over all examinees.[2] Whenever the test includes the use of recordings, the size and acoustical characteristics of the testing room are of particular importance: if the room is large, the examinees will not all be hearing the recorded stimulus in the same way, and there may be interference from echo. For such tests it is definitely better to use two or more small or medium-sized rooms than one large auditorium.[3]

Most tests require a good deal of writing space. This is particularly true of multiple-choice tests, which generally use separate test books and answer sheets. Individual tables or desks are obviously ideal; if these are not available, chairs must have arms on which examinees can write. Having students hold all their materials on their laps is extremely unsatisfactory and will almost certainly affect test results.

Provision must also be made for left-handed examinees, and they must be seated in such a position that their work cannot be seen by those to the left of or behind them.

2. **Checking materials and equipment.** At least a day in advance of the test—and considerably earlier if materials must be ordered from an outside source—the examiner must take a careful count of

[2] For a small group of examinees—say, up to about 25—no proctors are required. But if the number much exceeds 25, the examiner will need assistance in seating the examinees, distributing and collecting the test materials, replacing broken or dull pencils, and keeping order. A reasonable proctor-examinee ratio might be one proctor for each 50 examinees after the first 25.

[3] It should here be noted that auditoriums with rows of seats at different heights generally make unsatisfactory testing rooms because of the difficulty of seating candidates so that they cannot see the papers of those in front of them.

all testing materials to ensure that an adequate supply is available. He should have a few extra copies of all the examinees' supplies for use in case of emergencies, e.g., the arrival of an additional candidate, the replacement of a defective copy or of an answer sheet that an examinee has begun to mark in an improper way. If reusable test books are being used, the examiner must check for, and discard, marked copies. If pencils are to be supplied to the examinees, the quantity available must be sufficient to provide for a goodly number of replacements. And even if candidates are asked to bring their own pens or pencils, it must be assumed that some additional ones will be needed.

If use is to be made of audio equipment, the examiner must (1) ensure that the machines are in good working condition, (2) play through the tapes or records to see that they are of satisfactory quality, and (3) check on the location of electrical outlets in the testing room and obtain any necessary extension cords. Indeed, the only safe procedure is for the examiner, assisted if possible by the proctors, to try out the equipment in the testing room prior to the administration. In this way he can make certain that the sound will be clear in all parts of the room and can select the most effective setting for the volume.

Finally, the examiner must obtain an accurate watch for timing the test. For precise timing, this watch should have a sweep second hand and easy-to-read numbers. He should also arrange for a second timepiece to be available for emergency use in the event of the failure of his own. Perhaps one of the proctors will have a suitable watch and help the examiner keep time. In addition to the above, it is extremely helpful to have a wall clock in the testing room by which the examinees can check their own time. If none is available, the examiner should either supply a large clock himself (for a small or medium-sized room, an ordinary alarm clock will do) or be prepared to post the time periodically on a blackboard.

3. **Reading the test materials in advance.** The examiner must familiarize himself with all the test materials in advance of the administration. If an examiner's manual is provided, he must read this carefully and take special note of the timing. If he is required to read test directions aloud, he should practice these and try to anticipate questions that examinees might raise.

If several subtests are to be given, the examiner must decide at what point (if any) a rest period will be given. And if there is no established order for the subtests, he must decide upon the most appropriate sequence. (If, for example, there are two short subtests and one long one, it is normally best to give the two short subtests first, then have the rest period, and finally administer the long subtest. If one of the subtests involves concentrated listening to tapes or records, it is wise to administer this part of the test before the examinees have grown tired.)

CONDUCTING THE TESTING PRELIMINARIES

1. **Seating the examinees.** As the examinees arrive at the testing room, the proctors should have them take alternate seats within rows. If possible, empty rows should be left between examinees, but in any case examinees should be seated in a direct line with those in front of them. In the following plan, the x's indicate the seats to which small numbers of examinees should be assigned, and the asterisks mark additional seats that may be used if necessary. (It is assumed that there is a center aisle of sufficient width to prevent examinees in aisle seats from looking across at each others' papers. If the aisle is narrow, it would be well to leave the aisle seats on one side or the other vacant.)

Seating arrangement

[x]	[ ]	[x]	[ ]	[x]		[x]	[ ]	[x]	[ ]	[x]
[*]	[ ]	[*]	[ ]	[*]		[*]	[ ]	[*]	[ ]	[*]
[x]	[ ]	[x]	[ ]	[x]		[x]	[ ]	[x]	[ ]	[x]
[*]	[ ]	[*]	[ ]	[*]		[*]	[ ]	[*]	[ ]	[*]
[x]	[ ]	[x]	[ ]	[x]		[x]	[ ]	[x]	[ ]	[x]

All examinees should be assigned to their seats in a random order to prevent friends from sitting near each other according to a prearranged cheating plan.

2. **Calling the examination to order.** When the examinees have all

been seated, the examiner should call the group to order and briefly introduce the test. A calm, unhurried, yet businesslike manner can help put examinees at ease while at the same time establishing a good working atmosphere. The precise way in which the test is introduced will, of course, depend in large part on the nature of the test itself. Certainly, however, in his opening remarks the examiner should (a) emphasize the need for absolute quiet throughout the testing period, (b) explain under what circumstances the examinees should summon a proctor, and (c) indicate what examinees should do if they complete the test before time is called.[4] If the testing session is to be a long one, the examinees should be told the overall schedule, including when a rest period will occur. The introductory remarks should conclude with instructions on handling the test materials that are about to be distributed (e.g., "You will now be given a test book and answer sheet. Do not open the test book until you are told to do so, and do not write anything on the answer sheet until I give you directions.").

3. **Distributing the test materials.** Following his introductory remarks, the examiner should signal the proctors to distribute the test materials. Materials should be given *individually* to each examinee. Inasmuch as most tests are secure, multiple copies should not be entrusted to any examinee for distribution, even within his own row.

4. **Instructing examinees on filling out the answer sheet.** When all materials have been distributed, the examiner should explain how the personal data portion of the answer sheet is to be filled out. (If answer sheets are not used, instructions should be given on signing the test books, composition paper, or whatever other materials the examinees will use for recording their responses.) During this explanation, the use of a blackboard is often helpful. Proctors should check to see that examinees understand and are following the examiner's instructions and are not looking at the test items.

5. **Giving test directions.** Clear, complete directions to examinees should be included in the test itself. If the test calls for these to be read aloud by the examiner, they should be read slowly and distinctly with no departures from the established wording. If the

---

[4]Ordinarily it is best to keep all examinees in their seats until time is called. Otherwise, the group is very likely to be disturbed by the activity that necessarily attends an individual's departure, and the slower examinees may be upset by seeing that someone has already completed the test.

test specifies that examinees may be allowed to ask questions about the directions, the directions may be paraphrased but must on no account be added to in any substantive way. If examples are not understood, they should be read again with a minimum of explanation; examiners should never improvise additional examples. And no questions not directly related to the directions or sample problems should be permitted.

CONDUCTING THE TEST

1. **Beginning and timing the test.** At the conclusion of the pre-liminaries, the examiner should pause briefly and then announce the start of the test (e.g., "Now open your test book to problem number 1 and *begin work*"); as he does so, he must start his timing.[5]

Probably the single greatest source of error during test adminis-trations is the improper timing of tests which have precise time limits. To ensure maximum test reliability and validity, the examiner must therefore (1) see that all examinees begin work together, (2) keep accurate time throughout the testing period, and (3) stop all examinees exactly on schedule. It has already been suggested that, as an additional safeguard, the examiner may wish to ask one of the proctors also to note the starting time so that he might later be consulted should something happen to the examiner's timepiece.

2. **Proctoring the test.** As soon as the actual test administration begins, the proctors should walk quietly around the room checking to see that examinees are marking their answers in the prescribed manner. If a candidate clearly has not understood how he is to answer the problems, the proctor should offer brief instructions in a soft voice. Throughout the testing period the proctors should frequently walk about the room to make sure that examinees are not cheating and, if the test has separately timed parts, to see that examinees are working only on the part assigned for that time period. Proctors should move as silently and unobtrusively as possible and never stand beside an examinee so long as to disturb or embarrass him. Proctors must at all times pay strict attention to their

---

[5] If a watch with a start-and-stop device is used, it is merely necessary to start the timer and of course check to see that it is working correctly. If the examiner is using an ordinary watch, he should set it at a convenient time (2:15 rather than 2:17), wait until the second hand is pointing exactly at "12," and then say "Begin work." He should then make a written note of the precise starting time. The above procedure should be repeated at the beginning of every timed section of the test.

duties; they should not read or engage in conversation with one another while the test is in progress.

No latecomers should be allowed to enter the room once the actual administration begins. If possible, the door should be locked; in any event, a proctor should go quickly to the door if anyone attempts to enter during testing, and discussion with latecomers should be conducted outside the testing room.

Whenever an examinee requests to go to the rest room during actual testing, the proctor should collect his test materials and return them to him upon his return. It is obviously inadvisable to allow more than one examinee to be gone at the same time; if it becomes absolutely necessary, a proctor should accompany them.

Instances of cheating or other irregularities which proctors observe should be reported at once to the examiner, who should remain at his desk at the front of the room. It is the examiner's responsibility to make decisions about the handling of serious irregularities. (In the case of obvious cheating it is the usual procedure to collect the examinee's materials at once and dismiss him.) Any irregularities occurring during testing (unexpected interruptions which affect the timing of the test, the dismissal of examinees because of illness or as a disciplinary measure, etc.) should be recorded in writing by the examiner. These notes may later prove extremely useful in interpreting test results. (In most large-scale testing programs, examiners are required to fill out a report form noting such irregularities and submit the form when the answer sheets are returned to the organization for scoring.)

3. Concluding the test. When the testing time is exactly up, the examiner should call time (e.g., *"Stop work on the test.* Put down your pencils and close your test books."). Proctors should check quickly to see that these directions have been followed by all examinees.[6] Examinees should then be told to remain quietly in their seats until all the test materials are collected and counted. The proctors should then take the materials from each examinee individually and assist the examiner in counting them. When the examiner is sure that he has a full set from each examinee, he may dismiss the group.

---

[6]If there is a rest period after one section of the test, the examinees should be directed to place their answer sheets inside the test books and leave the books closed on their desks. A short rest period (preferably about five minutes) may then be announced, during which the examinees may stand by their seats and talk quietly. It is generally wise not to allow the examinees to leave the room during the rest period because of the problem of reassembling them all promptly at the end of the "break."

11 Interpreting and Using Test Results

THE INTERPRETATION OF SCORES

Raw Scores

Raw scores are obtained simply by counting the number of right answers. A raw score as such has very limited meaning; without other information we cannot tell whether a raw score of, let us say, 50 out of 100 possible points represents superior, average, or poor performance. A simple example will illustrate the point. Ordinarily, we might suppose that a raw score of 24 out of 26 would be excellent, while a score of 12 out of 26 would be quite low. But if, as part of a test of mental control, a group of college graduates were asked to name the letters of the alphabet in proper sequence, a score of 24 right out of 26 would hardly qualify as excellent. If, on the other hand, another section of the test called for these same subjects to recite the letters of the alphabet in *reverse* order within very narrow time limits, a score of 12 out of 26 might very well have a rating of superior.

It would seem a truism, therefore, that a raw score *without context* can have little real meaning. Yet the superstition persists that raw scores *do* have significance in themselves, and many a teacher has been confronted by a disgruntled student whose argument runs, "I got 50 right out of 100, and *everybody knows* that 50 is passing." (It would seem that, in our Western culture at least, 50 has joined such time-honored magic numbers as 3 and 7.)

How, then, are we to give meaning to raw scores? Obviously, for each test we must have some simple method of interpreting raw scores in terms of the general performance of some group or groups. One method is to determine the "average" score on the test so that each subject's performance may be compared with the "average." Another way is to convert the raw scores into percentile or standard scores in order to show approximately *how far* above or below the "average" each subject's score is. Let us consider briefly each of these kinds of calculations and some of the ways in which statisticians use them to describe tests and report scores.

Measures of Central Tendency

It has perhaps been noted that whenever the term *average* was used above, it was safely tucked between quotation marks. The reason for this is that the term has no one universal meaning; there are several kinds of averages, or "measures of central tendency," to use the statistician's phrase. Two of these are so commonly used in testing that they should be thoroughly understood by all users of tests.

The *median* is the midpoint of a series of scores when the scores are arranged in order of their size. Let us say that fifteen students have obtained these test scores: 52, 34, 29, 48, 59, 20, 29, 41, 51, 40, 35, 27, 44, 51, 38. To determine the median, we first arrange these raw scores in ascending order of size: 20, 27, 29, 29, 34, 35, 38, 40, 41, 44, 48, 51, 51, 52, 59. Now we find the midpoint of the series, which in the case of our 15 scores would be the eighth score from either end. We find that the midpoint score, the median, is 40.

The *arithmetic mean*, often shortened to the *mean,* is the sum of the separate scores divided by their number. If we add together the fifteen scores given in the previous paragraph, our total will be 598. If we then divide 598 by 15, the number of scores we have, the mean is 39.87.

In the example given above, the median and the mean were nearly equivalent because the scores tended to cluster fairly symmetrically around a central point. But consider the following series of 15 scores: 35, 36, 37, 40, 41, 43, 45, 46, 48, 48, 49, 52, 54, 96, 98. Two of the examinees apparently found this a much easier test than did the others, and because of them the mean, 51.20, is of a greater value than 11 of the 15 scores in the sample. Obviously here the median would give us a much better notion of the "average" than would the mean.

When, however, a test maker reports an "average score" for his test, he is generally basing his statistics on a pretty large sample—at least 100 scores, perhaps several hundred. In such cases the distribution of scores is likely to be fairly symmetrical, and he will probably calculate the mean, the statistic which takes full account of every value in his sample.

When working with large numbers of scores, the statistician uses shortcut procedures to determine the mean (or median). The reader who desires to acquaint himself with these techniques is referred to the next chapter. Here we shall only point out that when a large sample is used, the scores are arranged in a *frequency distribution* of the type shown in columns 1 and 2 of Table 1. It will be noted that, for simplicity, scores are here arranged in five-point intervals—though

Table 1. Frequency Distribution and Percentile Ranks
for English Structure Test Scores for 100 Foreign Students

(1)	(2)	(3)
		Percentile
Scores	Frequency	ranks
95-99	2	99
90-94	3	97
85-89	4	93
80-84	6	88
75-79	7	82
70-74	9	74
65-69	11	64
60-64	14	51
55-59	12	38
50-54	10	27
45-49	8	18
40-44	5	12
35-39	4	7
30-34	3	4
25-29	2	1

two-, three-, four-, and even ten-point groups are also frequently employed. The mean of the sample shown in Table 1 is 61.90; the median is 61.64.

The Standard Deviation (SD)

As pointed out above, the chief value of a measure of central tendency is to provide us with a concise indication of the typical test performance of a total group of examinees. With such data we may compare an individual's performance with that of his fellow examinees, or we may compare two or more groups in terms of typical performance on a given test. It is always important, therefore, for test makers to provide information about the "average" score or scores which have been obtained.

Yet a moment's reflection will reveal the need for some further data. Let us suppose that a test of 80 items has been administered and that the mean score is found to have been 40. We have no way of knowing, from this statistic, what the range or spread of the test scores may have been. The most obvious way of indicating the range would be to give the highest and lowest scores; let us say that, in our test of 80 items, the highest and lowest scores obtained were 78 and 15 respectively. Such statistics, however, are extremely crude and are apt to be deceptive. Perhaps only one examinee in a hundred scored above 50, and only one member of the group scored below 30. In such a case, our range of 78 to 15 would give a most misleading picture of test performance.

The *standard deviation* (often abbreviated to *SD* or symbolized with a lower-case sigma) is the most stable "index of variability" (i.e., measure of the range of scores) and is customarily employed in statistical reports of test performance. We shall not endeavor, in this brief summary, to detail the procedures for calculating the standard deviation; the reader who is interested in these will find them described in the next chapter.[1] More important for our present purposes is an understanding of what the standard deviation should mean to us when we find it in a test report.

It is first necessary to understand that educational test scores tend to be distributed symmetrically about their means in pro-

---

[1] Briefly, in the computation of the standard deviation, each individual's deviation from the group mean is squared; the standard deviation is then found by taking the square root of the mean of these squares.

portions which approximate those of the "normal probability curve." If, therefore, we assume that the scores on a given test will be so distributed, we may interpret the standard deviation as follows:

1. 68 percent of the scores will fall within one *SD* above and one *SD* below the mean.
2. An additional 27 percent of the scores will fall within the second *SD* above and below the mean; that is, 2 *SD*'s above and 2 *SD*'s below the mean will include 95 percent of the cases or scores.
3. Three *SD*'s above and below the mean will include over 99 percent—virtually all—of the scores.[2]

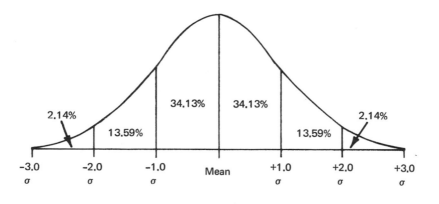

Figure 6. Normal Probability Curve

A specific example may help to clarify the use of the standard deviation. Let us suppose that a test maker has accumulated the data shown in columns 1 and 2 of Table 1 and wishes to provide the users of his test with a brief summary of his sampling of scores without actually including the whole frequency-distribution table. He will tell us that the highest possible score on the test is 100, that the mean of the scores for 100 examinees of such-and-such a type was 61.90, and that the standard deviation of this sample was 15.98. What practical use may we make of this last statistic?

First, as suggested above, the standard deviation tells us whether the test scores tend to bunch together or are distributed more or less evenly over a broad range. If the purpose of the test is to measure

[2] All the above percentages were rounded off. See Fig. 6 for more exact calculations.

several levels of proficiency or attainment, we shall want a broad range of scores. If, on the other hand, the purpose of the test is, for example, simply to predict which students will succeed and which will fail in some academic task, then a broad, symmetrical spread of scores becomes less crucial. (The standard deviation for the data presented in Table 1 indicates a fairly broad score range.)

Secondly, the standard deviation gives us a better basis than simply the mean for interpreting individual scores. Let us say that a subject has received a score of 80 on the English structure test and we wish to determine how his performance would compare with that of the subjects who comprised the above sample. We can quickly determine that one standard deviation above our mean of 61.90 is 77.88 (by adding one standard deviation, 15.98, to the mean of 61.90). Provided that the distribution of scores approaches the symmetry illustrated in Figure 6, we may assume that a score of 80 is superior to at least 83.99 percent of the scores in the sample. If the examinees in the sample group were fairly similar (in training, experience, vocational interests, and the like) to our candidate with his 80, we may conclude that the latter has done quite well on the test.

Percentile Ranks

Means and medians, as pointed out above, give us an idea of the typical performance on a test; they cannot tell us how much above or below the "average" a particular score may be. The standard deviation, as we have seen, is therefore useful in providing a kind of general context in which to interpret scores. Often, however, we need more specific data on the ranking of individual test performances. One procedure is to translate all the raw scores into *percentile ranks* whereby we may gain a fairly clear notion of the relative standing of each examinee with respect to the others. A subject's percentile rank indicates the percent of the group which *scored lower* on the test than he did. Thus, if we find that an individual's score of 92 gives him a percentile rank of 97 on the test, we know that he did better than 97 percent of the examinees in the comparison group. With a knowledge of percentile ranks, we may quickly compile lists of those examinees who are in the upper fourth of their group, and so on. Percentile ranks are also useful when we wish to compare the standing of an individual on one test with his standing on another. And by computing percentile ranks for a large collection of scores (several hundred at least), we may develop a set of *local norms* with which subsequent individual performances can then be compared. Column 3 in Table 1 shows the conversion of the raw scores to percentile ranks.

A characteristic weakness of percentile scores may be observed in the data of Table 1: the marked inequality of percentile units, particularly at the extremes of the distribution. Thus, for example, a student who raised his raw score from 50 to 60 would improve his percentile ranking by about 24 points, while another student whose raw score increased from 80 to 90 would pick up only about 9 percentile-rank points. Yet the actual accomplishment of the latter student—his skills growth—might be far more significant than that of the former. The explanation of this lies, as we have observed above, in the tendency of test scores to bunch around the center of a distribution and thin out at the ends, as seen in the "normal probability curve" in Figure 6.

Standard Scores

To remedy the defect of unequal units which we noted above in connection with percentile ranks, and to provide a scoring system which will permit a more meaningful direct comparison of the results of one test administration with the results of another, many test makers now employ *standard scores* by which raw scores are converted to a special scale having a constant mean and standard deviation. Thus, for example, the College Entrance Examination Board converts the raw scores on its examinations to a scale with 500 as the mean and 100 as the standard deviation.[3] In interpreting the scores for these tests, therefore, we can assume that about two-thirds of the candidates in any large administration will score between 400 and 600 (one standard deviation below and above the mean) and that the remaining cases will fall below and above these points in the proportions shown in Figure 6 on page 125. Quite obviously, such a system assumes that the distribution of scores will closely approximate the "normal probability curve," and for this reason the original scaling must be based upon a very large sample.

---

[3]Other commonly used scales have a mean of 50 and a *SD* of 10, or a mean of 100 and a *SD* of 20.

SOME SPECIAL FACTORS AFFECTING SCORES

The Effect of Guessing

One of the commonly debated questions in multiple-choice testing is whether or not to compensate statistically for chance guessing. Where a statistical correction for guessing is applied, the procedure is usually the following:

Number of item choices	Correction for guessing
5	Score = no. right minus 1/4 no. wrong
4	Score = no. right minus 1/3 no. wrong
3	Score = no. right minus 1/2 no. wrong
2	Score = no. right minus no. wrong

The rationale of the above is easily understood. If a test consists, for example, of one hundred 4-choice items, a subject who answered all 100 items by marking choice A would probably get about one-fourth of the items, or 25, correct. If his score were then computed by taking the number right, 25, and subtracting one-third of 75, the number he got wrong, he would be left with a score of zero. Thus he would have gained no advantage whatever from his attempts at "beating the game" through blind guessing.

It is readily apparent, however, that the candidates who did *not* guess would be unduly penalized for their wrong answers. Thus, in the same test a fair student whose "true" score should have been 50 would, through the application of the statistical correction for guessing, receive a score of only 33.

Inasmuch as there is no general agreement among statisticians on how the problem of guessing should be treated, no final answers can be offered here. The following points simply represent the writer's own opinions.

1. The subjects who take tests of English as a second language will very seldom attempt to guess their way through. Therefore, correction for guessing tends to overcompensate for what little blind guessing there actually is.

2. If a test consists of 4- or 5-choice items, even an extreme case of chance guessing would probably not affect the score significantly. (For instance, in our example above, the score obtained by guessing

one's way through one-hundred 4-choice items is only 25, which normally would not be an acceptable score.) Therefore, correction for guessing would generally seem unnecessary in a test with items of this sort.

3. If, however, a test consists of 3-choice items (and occasionally the nature of the test material seems to prohibit more choices), scores obtained by chance guessing would tend to run high enough to be fairly significant. In this case, correction for guessing can certainly be justified.

4. Whenever possible, 2-choice items should be avoided because of the very strong effect on scores which blind guessing will have. And if the correction-for-guessing formula is applied to all papers, a great injustice will be worked on examinees who do not blind-guess. (For example, a conscientious student of somewhat limited competence who answers all the 2-choice items to the best of his ability and should obtain a score near the 50 percent mark will, through the application of the traditional formula, be left with a final score near zero.)   This is one of the reasons why the familiar true-false tests are regarded as suspect by many testing specialists, except perhaps when used for pedagogical purposes—as in informal classroom tests as part of instruction.

5. Whether or not chance guessing is statistically compensated for, the test directions should make it very clear that guessing is or is not penalized. If there is a correction for guessing, the directions might say: "If you do not know the answer to a question, do not guess, for guessing will lower your score." If there is no penalty for guessing, the directions might read: "Try to answer every question even if you are not sure your answer is correct. Your score will be the number of questions you get right."

6. Different individuals respond differently to the challenge of guessing. The brash candidate who enjoys a gamble will have no inhibitions whatsoever about guessing. The cautious subject, on the other hand, may find it very painful, if not downright impossible, to answer items he is not sure of. Similarly, the various national groups may have very strong cultural attitudes about guessing. Therefore, scores on tests administered on a worldwide basis will inevitably reflect these attitudes and biases regardless of how the problem of guessing is treated by the test maker.

The Effect of Changing Answers

It would appear to be the popular notion that examinees should stick to their first decisions when answering test questions—that changing answers will tend to reduce one's score. Yet research has produced evidence that, "contrary to popular myth, students generally increase rather than lower their test scores when they reconsider and revise their original answers."[4] For example, an analysis of 930 answer-sheet corrections made by foreign students taking multiple-choice tests of English as a second language showed that 71 percent of the changes were from a wrong to a right answer.[5] It is questionable whether test administrators should stress this point when giving advice to examinees. On the other hand, however, it would be unwise and misleading to advise candidates *against* changing their original responses.

"Practice Effect"

Generally speaking, the more often we perform an operation, the more proficient we become at it. This is as true of test-taking as it is of driving a car or baking a cake. Thus we may expect subjects who are repeating a test (whether with the same or a parallel form) to score somewhat higher than they did the first time, even if their knowledge of the subject being tested has not itself increased. Test users must therefore make allowance for "practice effect" when evaluating scores on "progress" or "exit" tests; slight improvements in such scores quite possibly represent improvement in test-taking skills, not increased competence in subject-matter skills.

"Coaching Effect"

Somewhat related to the above is what might be called "coaching effect," that is, the effect on test scores of "teaching to the test." The question of how much coaching will affect scores has been the

[4] Robert L. Ebel and Dora E. Damrin, "Tests and Examinations," in Chester W. Harris (ed.), *Encyclopedia of Educational Research*, 3 ed. New York: The Macmillan Company,1960, p. 1512.

[5] The students were attending the American Language Institute of Georgetown University and took the *English Usage Test* (3-choice items) and the *Vocabulary and Reading Test* (4-choice items) developed by the institute. As might be expected, the percentage of wrong-to-right corrections was greater for the test with 3-choice items than for the test with 4-choice items: 75 and 66 percent, respectively.

subject of considerable research, but the conclusions of the studies have tended to be somewhat contradictory. The following would, however, seem to be safe generalizations.

1. Whenever test results are crucial to the future careers of large numbers of individuals, we must expect coaching to take place. (In the United States, coaching for College Board examinations has been a commonplace for years. Abroad, many schools and institutes in various parts of the world offer "courses" to prepare applicants for *TOEFL* and other standard tests of English as a second language.)

2. Whether intensive coaching will improve a student's test scores or not depends in large part on the *time interval* between coaching and testing. If the student is tested within a few months after studying for the test, his score may very well be affected to some degree. A long time lag, however, will tend to cancel out the effects of the training.

3. In places where the very mechanics of objective test-taking are generally unfamiliar to the population, some of the effects of coaching will simply be due to the student's becoming familiarized with the techniques. (Such coaching effect, which is really akin to practice effect, could be largely nullified by providing all applicants with a short practice test similar in all respects to the real test.)

"Test Compromise"

Very different from the above is "test compromise," the acquisition of prior knowledge of test content. Tests and test answers may be acquired by unauthorized persons in a number of ways: the test books or scoring keys may be stolen, or each of a group of examinees may memorize a certain number of items according to a prearranged plan so as to reconstruct the test later.

Particularly in the case of standard tests used to make crucial decisions about candidates, attempts at such compromise are almost inevitable. The best safeguard would be to have very infrequent test administrations—perhaps once or twice a year—using a new form with every administration. When such a system is not feasible, a sufficient number of forms must be available to make test memorization too formidable a task for the applicants. And the forms must be frequently rotated in a manner which cannot be predicted by the test-takers. Finally, it goes without saying that tests, keys, and answer sheets must be kept as secure as is humanly possible.

TEST SCORES AS EVIDENCE OF SKILLS IMPROVEMENT

Tests are often used to measure student progress in acquiring certain knowledge or skills. In such cases either the same test or parallel forms of a test are administered at both the commencement and the conclusion of a study or training program. In using tests for this purpose, one should keep the following points in mind:

1. As has been emphasized throughout this book, to be really effective as a measure of achievement, a test must be based specifically upon the materials used in the particular study or training program which the subjects have undergone. For this reason, many general *proficiency* tests are of only limited usefulness as measures of *achievement*.

2. Also as noted above, some increases in test scores may be due largely or entirely to "practice effect," and slight changes—either up or down—may be due to the ever-present "error of measurement."

3. Generally speaking, the greatest improvement in test scores will be achieved by individuals who begin a study or training program at a low level of proficiency. This does not necessarily mean that the more advanced students gained little from the training or study; it may reflect the limitations of a single test, or set of tests, designed to measure subjects at all proficiency levels.[6]

THE PREPARATION AND USE OF EXPECTANCY TABLES

When an effective test—one that is internally sound and is appropriate in terms of the content and goals of the instructional program—has been used over a period of time to screen students entering a particular course or program of study, the scores can be used to make predictions about students' subsequent performance in the course or study program. First it is necessary to have the test scores and later course grades or other performance ratings for a large

---

[6]Thus, for example, an analysis of test scores for foreign students attending the American Language Institute of Georgetown University showed that those who entered with scores between 30 and 69 on the institute's *English Usage Test* increased their scores by an average of 18 points in two months' time, while students with entrance scores of 70 and above averaged test-score improvements of only 8 points after the same length of study. (It should be pointed out, however, that this test is designed as a measure of general proficiency and therefore is somewhat unsatisfactory when used as an achievement test.)

number of students from past years. These data are then entered on an *expectancy table* in which each student's original test score and subsequent grade are recorded in a single "cell." An example of such an expectancy table is shown in Table 2A. By reading the table both horizontally and vertically, one can find how students with certain test scores were subsequently graded. Suppose, for example, that a student scored 88 on the screening test and later received a grade of B in the course. His test score locates him in the second row from the top, and his course grade in the second column from the right. We see from the table that he was one of 18 students scoring in the 80s on the test and receiving a B at the end of the course. It will be observed that B was by far the most common course grade for students with entrance test scores in the 80s.

These data may be made somewhat easier to interpret by converting the numbers of students to percents, as shown in Table

Table 2. Two Forms of Expectancy Tables
Showing the Relation between Screening Test Scores
and Subsequent Course Grades for 200 Students

A

Test scores	Number receiving each grade				
	F	D	C	B	A
90-99				4	12
80-89			2	18	8
70-79			20	16	2
60-69		4	39	10	
50-59	1	10	15		
40-49	2	16	2		
30-39	6	6			
20-29	7				

B

Test scores	Percentage receiving each grade				
	F	D	C	B	A
90-99				25	75
80-89			7	64	29
70-79			53	42	5
60-69		7	74	19	
50-59	4	38	58		
40-49	10	80	10		
30-39	50	50			
20-29	100				

2B.   Here it can be quickly ascertained that 64 percent of the students who scored in the 80s on the test later obtained a B in their course of study.

If the same test continues to be used, and if there is no substantial change in the nature of either the student body or the course of instruction, we can use the table to make predictions about the probable class performance of new students on the basis of their initial test scores. We may predict, for example, that students receiving test scores in the 80s have, to judge from past records, about two chances in three of obtaining B's in the course for which they were screened. The data from the table might be further simplified and generalized as follows:

Test scores	Probable class performance
80-100	Good to excellent
60-79	Average to good
50-59	Poor to average
0-49	Poor

The value of such information to a school counselor is immediately apparent. The data of an expectancy table must, however, be interpreted with care: they can help us to talk about probabilities, but not about certainties. Our table does not, for instance, mean that *no* student scoring in the 50s on the screening test will do above average work in class. We can say only that, *to judge from past experience*, students with scores in the 50s will be most likely to receive course grades of C or under.

12

Computing Some
Basic Test Statistics

Relatively few teachers of English as a second language have received training in educational measurement, and undoubtedly to many, like the author, the recollections of high school and college courses in mathematics are still somewhat painful. Yet as we have tried to show in this book, there are certain basic statistical techniques that are highly useful to the language teacher who writes tests—even the informal tests of the classroom. Fortunately, anyone who has survived ninth-grade math can perform the simple computations that these techniques require. It is hoped, therefore, that the reader—whatever his mathematical training—will continue undaunted through Chapter 12 and, moreover, will put these basic statistics to work, for they will enable him to learn a good deal more about the language measures that he employs in his classes.

The examples offered in this chapter are based on very small numbers of scores. In actual practice one would generally base his test statistics on larger samples. However, it seemed advisable to keep the numbers small both for purposes of clarity and as a strong suggestion that it is often worthwhile to analyze the results of even a single classroom testing.

ARRANGING SCORES IN A FREQUENCY DISTRIBUTION

Large numbers of scores are easiest to work with if they are organized in a *frequency distribution* like that shown in Table 3. Once the scores have been so arranged, such typical test statistics as the mean, standard deviation, median, and percentile ranks can easily be calculated.

Steps

1. Look through all the scores to determine the highest and the lowest. Subtract the lowest from the highest to obtain the *range* of scores.
2. Decide on convenient *score groups*—the size of the intervals into which the scores will be grouped. It is generally advisable to have about a dozen groups; therefore, one may divide the range obtained in step 1 by 12 to obtain a convenient score-group size. Commonly chosen intervals are 3, 5, and 10 units in length, though other intervals are also employed.
3. On a sheet of lined paper set up the score groups with the highest at the top and the lowest at the bottom. Be sure that these intervals do not overlap; if, for example, you had groups such as 0-5, 5-10, you would not know where to put a score of 5.
4. Tally the number of scores falling in each group.
5. Total the number of tallies for each score group and enter in a column headed *frequency* (*f*).

Example

Suppose you had administered a 60-item test to a class of 40 students whose scores were then found to run from 57 down to 4. Subtracting 4 from 57 gives a range of 53. To determine a convenient score-group size, you would then divide 53 by 12, obtaining 4.4. A convenient interval size would be 5 units, with a top score group of 55-59. The remaining groups would be set up as shown in Table 3. For each of the 40 scores, you would then enter a tally beside the appropriate score group. When you had entered all the tallies, you would probably wish to total the tallies for each score group and express the total as an arabic numeral.

Table 3. Frequency Distribution of the Scores
for 40 Foreign Students on a Listening Comprehension Test

Score groups	Tallies	Frequency
55-59	/	1
50-54	//	2
45-49	//	2
40-44	///	3
35-39	////	4
30-34	7𝐻𝐿 /	6
25-29	7𝐻𝐿 ////	9
20-24	7𝐻𝐿	5
15-19	///	3
10-14	///	3
5-9	/	1
0-4	/	1
		N = 40

CALCULATING THE MEAN BY THE SHORT METHOD

As pointed out in the previous chapter, the mean is the most frequently used measure of central tendency in test statistics. To calculate the mean of a large number of scores, first arrange the scores in a frequency distribution and then proceed as follows.

Steps

1. Assume a mean at or near the center of the distribution, preferably on the score group containing the largest frequency. This *assumed mean* (*AM*) is expressed as the *midpoint* of the score group.
2. Count up from the score group containing the *AM*, calling the next higher score group +1, the one above that +2, etc.; similarly, count down (-1, -2, -3, etc.) from your arbitrary starting point, entering these positive and negative interval steps in the x' column. The score group containing the *AM* itself will be entered as zero.
3. Multiply each deviation (x') by its frequency (f) to obtain fx'.
4. Find the sum of the plus and minus fx', and divide this sum by the number of scores (N). This gives the correction (c) in terms of score groupings.

5. Multiply c by the interval length of the score groups (i) to obtain ci, the score correction.
6. Add ci algebraically to the *AM* to get the *actual mean* (*M*). (Sometimes ci will be positive and sometimes negative, depending upon where the mean was assumed in step 1.)

Example

Table 4 shows the calculation of the mean of the 40 scores which we earlier arranged in a frequency distribution. (Ignore column 5 for now; it will be used in the calculation of the standard deviation.) In Table 4 the mean is assumed at score group 25-29 (midpoint: 27) because this score group is near the center of the distribution and contains the largest number of cases (9). Deviations above score group 25-29 are therefore positive and those below are negative. We

Table 4.   Calculation of the Mean
and Standard Deviation by the Short Method

(1) Score groups	(2) Frequency f	(3) Deviation x'	(4) fx'	(5) fx'^2
55-59	1	6	6	36
50-54	2	5	10	50
45-49	2	4	8	32
40-44	3	3	9	27
35-39	4	2	8	16
30-34	6	1	6	6
25-29	9	0	47	
20-24	5	-1	-5	5
15-19	3	-2	-6	12
10-14	3	-3	-9	27
5-9	1	-4	-4	16
0-4	1	-5	-5	25
	$N = 40$		-29	252

$AM = 27.00$ $\qquad c = \dfrac{\Sigma fx'}{N} = \dfrac{18}{40} = .45 \qquad c^2 = .2025$

$ci = \underline{\ 2.25\ }$ $\qquad i = 5$

$M = 29.25$ $\qquad ci = .45 \times 5 = 2.25$

$$SD = i\sqrt{\frac{\Sigma fx'^2}{N} - c^2} = 5\sqrt{\frac{252}{40} - .2025} = 12.35$$

find the algebraic sum of the plus and minus fx'; in this case, 47 - 29 = 18. Our result, 18, is then divided by 40, the number of scores, giving a correction in terms of score groups (c) of .45. This is then multiplied by 5, the length of each score-group interval (i), giving a score correction (ci) of 2.25. Because ci is positive, it is added to the AM (27.00), giving an actual mean (M) of 29.25.

CALCULATING THE STANDARD DEVIATION BY THE SHORT METHOD

As explained in the previous chapter, the standard deviation (SD) is a measure of variability calculated around the mean. Once we have calculated the mean from a frequency distribution, only a few additional steps are necessary to obtain the SD.

Steps

1. Calculate the mean by the method described above and shown in Table 4: that is, by assuming a mean and later applying the correction ci to give the actual mean.
2. Now add one further column (fx'^2 —column 5 in Table 4) by multiplying each x' by the corresponding fx'. Note that we get rid of negative values by multiplying negatives by negatives (-1 X -5 = +5; -2 X -6 = +12, etc.).
3. Find the sum (Σ) of the fx'^2 column ($\Sigma fx'^2$) and divide it by the number of scores (N).
4. Subtract c^2, the squared correction to the AM in terms of score groups, from the result of step 3.
5. Find the square root of the result of step 4.
6. Multiply the square root by the interval length of the score groups (i). The result is the standard deviation.

Example

In the earlier calculation of the mean of our 40 scores, the correction (c) was found to be .45. Thus c^2 is .2025. The SD is then calculated by dividing 252, the sum of the fx'^2 column, by 40, the number of cases (result: 6.30), subtracting .2025 (c^2) from this (result: 6.0975), obtaining the square root of the result (2.4693), and multiplying this figure by 5, the length of each score group (result: 12.35).

CALCULATING THE MEDIAN FROM A FREQUENCY DISTRIBUTION

Although, as noted in the last chapter, the mean is the most frequently reported measure of central tendency in test statistics, there are times when the median, the central point in the distribution, is more representative of "average" performance—for example, when the number of cases is small and there are large gaps in the distribution of scores. Like the mean, the median is usually calculated from a frequency distribution.

Steps

1. Find $N/2$, that is, one-half of the scores (N) in the distribution.
2. Working from the small end of the distribution, count off F, the scores necessary to reach the exact lower limit of the score group upon which the median lies (l).
3. Compute the number of additional scores necessary to reach $N/2$.
4. Divide the result of step 3 by the frequency (the number of scores) on the interval which contains the median (f_m).
5. Multiply the result of step 4 by the size of the score groups (i).
6. Add the result of step 5 to l to get the median (Mdn).

Example

Using the data given in Table 4, we find that the distribution contains 40 cases or scores; therefore the median of the distribution will be that point which has 20 scores on either side of it. This point will be within the score group 25-29, the exact lower limit of which is 24.5.[1] Seven scores are needed to reach the median point from the score group directly beneath. Inasmuch as score group 25-29

---

[1]The usual mathematical meaning of a score is an interval which extends from .5 below to .5 above the "face value" of the score. Thus the exact lower limit of 25 is 24.5; the exact upper limit would be 25.5

contains 9 scores, we divide 7 by 9 (result: .7778) and multiply by 5, the size of each score group. The result of this step, 3.8890, is then added to 24.5, putting the median at 28.39.

$$Mdn = l + \left(\frac{N/2 - F}{f_m}\right) i = 24.5 + \frac{20-13}{9} \times 5 = 28.39$$

where l = exact lower limit of the score group upon which the median lies

F = sum of all scores below l

f_m = frequency (number of scores) within the score group containing the median

i = size of each score group or interval

COMPUTING PERCENTILE RANKS

As we observed in the previous chapter, percentile ranks are commonly used to show how each examinee's test performance is related to the performance of the rest of the group. When large numbers of scores are involved, we again begin by preparing a frequency distribution, adding a further column showing the *cumulative frequency* for each score group, as shown in Table 5. The percentile rank for each score group is then computed as follows.

Steps

For each score group:

1. Find one-half the frequency of that group.
2. Add the result of step 1 to the cumulative frequency of the score group *just below* the one in question.
3. Divide the result of step 2 by the total number of scores (N), taking the answer to the nearest hundredth.
4. Multiply the result of step 3 by 100.

Note: For simplicity's sake, percentile ranks higher than 99 and lower than 1 may be treated as 99 and 1, respectively.

Table 5. Calculation of Percentile Ranks for Test Scores

Score groups	Frequency	Cumulative frequency	Percentile ranks
55-59	1	40	99
50-54	2	39	95
45-49	2	37	90
40-44	3	35	84
35-39	4	32	75
30-34	6	28	63
25-29	9	22	44
20-24	5	13	26
15-19	3	8	16
10-14	3	5	9
5-9	1	2	4
0-4	1	1	1

Example

Thus for score group 35-39 in Table 5, take one-half of 4, the frequency, and add the result (2) to 28 (the cumulative frequency of the score group just below), and divide the result (30) by 40, the total number of scores. The result is .75, which, multiplied by 100, gives 75.

CALCULATING THE COEFFICIENT OF CORRELATION FROM RANK ORDERS (RANK-DIFFERENCE METHOD)

The coefficient of correlation is a statistic which expresses the degree of relationship between two sets of test scores or other variables. It is useful to teachers who wish to determine, for example, how their students' performance on one test (say, a vocabulary test) corresponds to their performance on another (perhaps a grammar test) or who wish to see how performance on an entrance test correlates with subsequent course grades. As we saw in Chapter 2, test validity is often estimated by such comparisons.

Probably the most frequently employed technique for determining the correlation between two sets of test scores is by means of the Pearson product-moment formula. It is likely, however, that most teachers would find the computation of this statistic rather complicated. Fortunately, there is a much simpler method of calculating a correlation coefficient which is quite adequate when the numbers of scores are rather small (i.e., no more than about 30), as in the typical class of English as a second language. It is known as the *rank-difference* method and consists, as the name suggests, of determining the relationship between the way students are ranked on two tests.

Steps

1. Rank each student's performance on each of the two tests (1 = highest score, 2 = second highest score, etc.). In case of tied ranks, average the ranks (see the example below).
2. Find the difference (D) between each pair of ranks.
3. Square the differences (D^2).
4. Find the sum (Σ) of the D^2 column.
5. The result of step 4 (ΣD^2), together with N, the number of students, may now be put in the rank-difference formula to obtain the coefficient of correlation, ρ (*rho*):

$$\rho = 1 - \frac{6 \times \Sigma D^2}{N(N^2 - 1)}$$

Example

In Table 6, 15 students have been ranked on two tests. Note that because both Gomez and Torres stood in second place on Test A, each was given a rank of 2.5, and the student next in rank, Bu, was given the rank of 4. Likewise, on Test B there was a three-way tie for second place: Diegas, Ho, and Montero. Therefore, each of these students (who occupied ranks 2, 3, and 4) was given the median rank of 3. Gomez, the student next in line in Test B, received a rank of 5.

Next the difference between each pair of ranks was entered in the D column. Each difference was then squared (D^2 column); the sum of these squared differences (ΣD^2) was 165.50, the fraction of course resulting from the two-way tie on Test A.

Then 165.50 was multiplied by 6 (result: 993). The number of students, 15, was then multiplied by 15^2 minus 1 (224), giving 3,360. Finally, 993 was divided by 3,360, and the result (.2955) was subtracted from 1 to obtain the coefficient of correlation .7045.

Table 6. Calculation of the Correlation between Two Sets of Test Scores by the Rank-difference Method

Students	Ranks on Test A	Ranks on Test B	Difference in ranks (D)	D^2
Bu	4.0	1.0	3.0	9.00
Chin	8.0	11.0	3.0	9.00
Diegas	5.0	3.0	2.0	4.00
Fan	12.0	9.0	3.0	9.00
Gomez	2.5	5.0	2.5	6.25
Ho	9.0	3.0	6.0	36.00
Kim	14.0	15.0	1.0	1.00
Lamas	1.0	6.0	5.0	25.00
Montero	6.0	3.0	3.0	9.00
Park	15.0	12.0	3.0	9.00
Ramirez	10.0	13.0	3.0	9.00
Sung	13.0	10.0	3.0	9.00
Torres	2.5	7.0	4.5	20.25
Vargas	7.0	8.0	1.0	1.00
Yu	11.0	14.0	3.0	9.00
				165.50

$$\rho = 1 - \frac{6 \times \Sigma D^2}{N(N^2 - 1)} = 1 - \frac{6 \times 165.50}{15 \times 224} = 1 - \frac{993}{3360} = .7045$$

ESTIMATING TEST RELIABILITY

In Chapter 2 we discussed reliability as one of the characteristics of a good test. Reliability, it will be remembered, refers to the consistency of the measure. A test is said to be reliable if its scores remain relatively stable from one administration to another. The techniques used by statisticians to estimate the reliability of a test are somewhat complicated, and most classroom teachers probably have neither the time nor the inclination to learn or use these procedures. Yet even in informal classroom testing it is important to have some notion of the reliability of one's measures, for no conscientious teacher would want to make crucial decisions about his students on the basis of definitely unreliable examinations.

Table 7 provides a shortcut method of estimating the reliability of a test simply on the basis of the number of items, the mean, and the standard deviation.

Steps

1. On the basis of the mean score, determine whether the test is

easy (mean score between 70 percent and 90 percent correct) or difficult (mean between 50 percent and 70 percent correct). If it is an easy test, use Table 7A; if it is a difficult test, use Table 7B.

Table 7. Estimating the Approximate Reliability of a Test[*]

A. Easy Test (Average 70 to 90% Correct)

Number of items (n)	20	30	40	50	60	70	80	90	100
If SD is .10n	.21	.48	.62	.69	.75	.78	.81	.83	.85
If SD is .15n	.68	.80	.84	.88	.90	.91	.92	.93	.94
If SD is .20n	.84	.90	.92	.94	.95	.96	.96	.97	.97

B. Difficult Test (Average 50 to 70% Correct)

Number of items (n)	20	30	40	50	60	70	80	90	100
If SD is .10n	—	.21	.41	.53	.61	.66	.71	.74	.77
If SD is .15n	.49	.67	.75	.80	.84	.86	.88	.89	.90
If SD is .20n	.74	.83	.87	.90	.92	.93	.94	.94	.95

[*]Taken from Paul B. Diederich, *Short-cut Statistics for Teacher-made Tests,* Evaluation and Advisory Service Series, No. 5, 2d ed., Princeton, N.J.: Educational Testing Service, 1964, p. 31. By permission of Educational Testing Service.

2. Divide the standard deviation (*SD*) of the test by the number of items (*n*). If the *SD* is nearest to 10 percent of the items, use line 1; if 15 percent, line 2; and if 20 percent, line 3.
3. Choose the column that is nearest to the number of items in the test. The figure at the intersection of the appropriate row (from step 2) and column will be the approximate reliability of the test.

Example

Let us suppose that a 60-item listening test has been administered to 200 examinees and has been found to have a mean score of 32.00 and a standard deviation of 9.25 points. Inasmuch as the mean represents only 53 percent correct, this is clearly a difficult test, and we shall use Table 7B. The *SD* (9.25) represents 15 percent of 60, the number of items (*n*) in the test; therefore, we shall use the second line of the table. By inspection of Table 7B, we find that our 60-item test has an approximate reliability of .84.

ESTIMATING THE STANDARD ERROR OF MEASUREMENT (SE_{meas})

As noted in Chapter 2, the standard error of measurement (SE_{meas}) is used to estimate the limits within which an examinee's obtained score on a test is likely to diverge from his true score. If we know the standard deviation (SD) and the estimated reliability (r_t) of a test, we may estimate the standard error by the formula

$$SE_{meas} = SD\sqrt{1 - r_t}$$

Example

If the SD of a test is 9.25 points and the reliability of the test is estimated to be .84, the SE_{meas} would be 3.70 score points:

$$
\begin{aligned}
SE_{meas} &= 9.25\sqrt{1 - .84} \\
&= 9.25\sqrt{.16} \\
&= 9.25 \times .4 \\
&= 3.70
\end{aligned}
$$

If, therefore, an individual's true score were 40 on this test, we could say that the odds were 19 to 1 that his obtained score would not exceed 47.4 or fall below 32.6 (i.e., would fall within two standard errors above or below his true score of 40).

Selected References

The number of texts and reference works which deal with statistics and educational measurement is legion, and one could easily compile a list of fifty or a hundred. In a book such as this, however, it would seem inappropriate and exceedingly unhelpful to deluge the reader with a mere flood of titles. Instead, the writer has purposely restricted himself to just a handful of works which he believes will provide the answers to most questions the classroom teacher might have about the principles and techniques of test construction and evaluation. Each of the books on the list has a bibliography or one or more reference lists which will lead the reader to other treatments should he wish to pursue his study of educational measurement still further.

Buros, Oscar Krisen (ed.). *The Sixth Mental Measurements Yearbook.* Highland Park, N.J.: The Griffin Press, 1965.
   The various editions of the *Yearbook* constitute a very extensive critical bibliography of standardized tests produced in the English-speaking world. The latest volume lists over 1,200 tests, mostly from the period 1959-1964, the tests of more general interest being covered by two or more reviews. In addition, over 500 books on measurement subjects are listed, many entries including excerpts from the reviews which appeared in professional journals.

Garrett, Henry E. *Statistics in Psychology and Education*, 5th ed. New York: Longmans, Green & Co., Inc., 1958.
   One of the very few "introductory" statistics texts which can actually be comprehended by the layman, even when studying on his own. Only those statistical techniques of practical value in educational and psychological testing have been included, their specific values and limitations always being clearly defined.

Green, John A. *Teacher-made Tests.* New York: Harper & Row, Publishers, Incorporated, 1963.
   A brief and very readable text for the classroom teacher, giving practical suggestions for planning and writing informal tests and

assigning course grades. Basic test statistics are confined to one chapter at the end.

Lado, Robert. *Language Testing: The Construction and Use of Foreign Language Tests.* New York: McGraw-Hill Book Company, 1961.
Primarily intended for teachers of foreign languages and of English as a second language. Beginning with a discussion of language and language learning, it proceeds to a consideration of how the various language skills may be tested. Techniques for measuring cross-cultural understanding are also proposed. Several chapters at the end deal with fundamental test statistics.

Lindquist, E. F. (ed.). *Educational Measurement.* Washington: American Council on Education, 1951.
The comprehensive reference work and textbook on the theory and techniques of educational measurement. Twenty authorities on testing have contributed chapters in the areas of their specialization. The level of difficulty varies from chapter to chapter, and many sections are most definitely not for the beginning student of tests and measurement.

Thorndike, Robert L., and Elizabeth Hagen. *Measurement and Evaluation in Psychology and Education,* 2d ed. New York: John Wiley & Sons, Inc., 1961.
A sound general survey of the field of testing, with informative treatments of such topics as the preparation of objective and essay examinations, the improvement of ratings, the technical aspects of marking and grading, and the use of norms. A wide variety of standardized tests are described briefly. One chapter is devoted to statistical techniques of fundamental use to the "novice."

Valette, Rebecca M. *Modern Language Testing: A Handbook.* New York: Harcourt, Brace & World, Inc., 1967.
Designed for the foreign language teacher, most of the illustrative items being in Spanish, French, and German. Beginning with a treatment of basic principles and procedures of language testing (including a chapter on simple statistical techniques), the manual continues with chapters on the testing of the various language skills, and of culture and literature. An appendix describes the most widely used commercial foreign language tests.

Index